TECUMSEH

Recent Titles in Greenwood Biographies

TECUMSEH

A Biography

Amy H. Sturgis

GREENWOOD BIOGRAPHIES

GREENWOOD PRESS
WESTPORT, CONNECTICUT • LONDON

Library of Congress Cataloging-in-Publication Data

Sturgis, Amy H., 1971–
  Tecumseh : a biography / by Amy H. Sturgis.
    p. cm. — (Greenwood biographies, ISSN 1540–4900)
  Includes bibliographical references and index.
  ISBN 978–0–313–34177–9 (alk. paper)
  1. Tecumseh, Shawnee Chief, 1768–1813.   2. Shawnee Indians — Kings and rulers—
Biography.   3. Shawnee Indians — Government relations.   I. Title.
  E99.S35T348   2008
  970.004'97—dc22
  [B]   2008002109

British Library Cataloguing in Publication Data is available.

Library of Congress Catalog Card Number: 2008002109

ISBN: 978–0–313–34177–9
ISSN: 1540–4900

First published in 2008

Greenwood Press, 88 Post Road West, Westport, CT 06881
An imprint of Greenwood Publishing Group, Inc.
www.greenwood.com

Printed in the United States of America

The paper used in this book complies with the
Permanent Paper Standard issued by the National
Information Standards Organization (Z39.48–1984).

10   9   8   7   6   5   4   3   2   1

*In loving memory of my mother's mother, my Meemie (1924–2007),
and my father's father, my PaPa (1923–2007)*

CONTENTS

Photo essay follows page 68

SERIES FOREWORD

In response to high school and public library needs, Greenwood developed this distinguished series of full-length biographies specifically for student use. Prepared by field experts and professionals, these engaging biographies are tailored for high school students who need challenging yet accessible biographies. Ideal for secondary school assignments, the length, format and subject areas are designed to meet educators' requirements and students' interests.

Greenwood offers an extensive selection of biographies spanning all curriculum-related subject areas including social studies, the sciences, literature and the arts, history and politics, as well as popular culture, covering public figures and famous personalities from all time periods and backgrounds, both historic and contemporary, who have made an impact on American and/or world culture. Greenwood biographies were chosen based on comprehensive feedback from librarians and educators. Consideration was given to both curriculum relevance and inherent interest. The result is an intriguing mix of the well-known and the unexpected, the saints and sinners from long-ago history and contemporary pop culture. Readers will find a wide array of subject choices from fascinating crime figures like Al Capone to inspiring pioneers like Margaret Mead, from the greatest minds of our time like Stephen Hawking to the most amazing success stories of our day like J. K. Rowling.

While the emphasis is on fact, not glorification, the books are meant to be fun to read. Each volume provides in-depth information about the subject's life from birth on through childhood, the teen years, and adulthood.

A thorough account relates family background and education, traces personal and professional influences, and explores struggles, accomplishments, and contributions. A timeline highlights the most significant life events against a historical perspective. Bibliographies supplement the reference value of each volume.

ACKNOWLEDGMENTS

My thanks go to Mariah Gumpert for inviting me to participate in this series and for guiding this project. I am indebted to those scholars and storytellers who have chronicled Tecumseh's tale over the years, especially John Sudgen, whose monumental work, *Tecumseh: A Life*, remains the foundation of any examination of the Shawnee chief.

I am grateful to Paige Carter at Belmont University's Lilah D. Bunch Library for her assistance. I thank my family, friends, colleagues, and students for their support. The Shire's Virginia Lórien has my gratitude for her enthusiastic editorial involvement. Most important, I thank my dear husband, Larry M. Hall, to whom I owe more than I can ever repay. Any errors remaining in this work are my own.

INTRODUCTION

The story of Tecumseh is more than the tale of one man. Tecumseh was a Shawnee who was born in a time of turmoil, became an influential leader of his people, and died while still at the height of his strength. But even during his lifetime, Tecumseh's personal story became intertwined with legend. His potency as an international figure drew from myth as well as reality—a point that did not escape Tecumseh, his allies, or his enemies, all of whom played roles in managing and manipulating the mystique that developed around him. In the nineteenth century, published works about Tecumseh were as likely to be heroic epic poems or highly imaginative novels as researched biographical accounts. Scholars in the twentieth and twenty-first centuries have sought to disentangle Tecumseh's reality from fiction, only to discover that Tecumseh's story can be fully understood only when both the man and the legend are taken into account.

This apparent paradox—that learning the *truth* about Tecumseh requires us to step beyond the *facts* about him—is only one contradiction of many we find while exploring Tecumseh's story. For example, Tecumseh is perhaps most popularly remembered as the revolutionary figure who called for the creation of a pan-tribal Native confederacy to resist westward expansion by the United States in the late eighteenth and early nineteenth centuries. While Tecumseh was perhaps the most successful and visible leader to champion pan-tribal unity as a form of resistance, he was not innovative for embracing this vision. In fact, he inherited a vibrant tradition for such action, dating back at least as far as the Ottawa leader Pontiac's rebellion against British occupation of the Great Lakes region after the French and Indian War and the Mohawk leader

Joseph Brant's efforts to create a confederation to oppose U.S. expansion into the Northwest Territory at the end of the colonies' War of Independence. Even among his own people, Tecumseh was not a pioneer; fellow Shawnees such as Blue Jacket and Captain Johnny sought to unify northwestern tribes to defend the Ohio region against the United States before him. Tecumseh's real achievement lay in imagining a more geographically expansive confederation than his predecessors had envisioned and in working toward making it a reality from Canada to Spanish Florida. Of course, being more personally charismatic, politically adept, and militarily savvy than those who came before him certainly did not hurt his cause.

Tecumseh's public and private relationship with his brother Tenskwatawa, the Prophet, introduces additional contradictions to Tecumseh's story. The Prophet's religious revitalization movement for a time worked in tandem with Tecumseh's goals for Native America. The Prophet's notoriety preceded and paved the way for Tecumseh's fame—some early U.S. reports identified Tecumseh only as the Prophet's brother—and the Prophet's call for a return to cultural purity and traditional faith complemented Tecumseh's message of resistance. The Prophet was not exactly a partner and fellow traveler with Tecumseh, however. It is a mistake to think of Tecumseh as handling the secular side of the pan-tribal movement while the Prophet led the spiritual side. First, many Native American cultures did not differentiate between the religious and the political in the same way some European societies did, and such a dichotomy would not have been meaningful to the Shawnees or their neighbors. Second, Tecumseh embraced the Prophet's teachings only up to a limit, and when they matched his own worldview. He approved of the Prophet's exhortation for American Indians to return to time-honored lifestyles and to reject U.S. influences, for example, but he disapproved of the Prophet's bloody witch hunts, intended to purify the native nations. Tecumseh harnessed the momentum of the Prophet's message to further his own, but when the Prophet disappointed him and lost credibility and favor with his people, Tecumseh disassociated himself from his brother and continued along his own consistent path. Alternately buoyed and embarrassed by the Prophet, Tecumseh's commitment to pan-tribal unity outweighed other concerns, including family unity.

An even more significant paradox appears when we consider Tecumseh's image as the symbol of "the Indian" alongside his actions as a resistance leader. For many people of his day, both indigenous Americans and U.S. citizens, Tecumseh embodied Native America. This is not surprising: he thought in terms not of Shawnees, for instance, but rather of American Indians as a whole, united against U.S. encroachment. He therefore pursued ways of minimizing the differences and maximizing the common ground among the native nations. He employed his sophisticated appreciation of symbolic behavior to these ends. At the height of his movement, he ate only what he considered to be indigenous foods and abstained from the "white man's" alcohol. He dressed plainly and conservatively in traditional style, presenting an archaic, unusual figure even to his people, as if history had come alive to show them how an Indian free of Anglo influences would look and behave. Many who adopted his vision followed his example.

Yet Tecumseh's behavior does not represent the actions of a classic separatist or purist, of "the native" pitted against "the imperialist." On the contrary, Tecumseh followed a shrewd policy of *realpolitik*, seeking his way by international negotiation as well as war and ultimately allying himself with the former colonizer Great Britain against the United States. He trusted, respected, and worked closely with men of backgrounds different from his own, such as the British Indian agent Matthew Elliott and the British major-general Isaac Brock. Tecumseh proved himself to be an able politician as well as soldier on the stage of British/U.S. affairs. His performance as an ally, in fact, earned him the status of Canadian national hero, as well as Native American icon. Therefore, even as he was considered the epitome of the Native American, Tecumseh also became known as "the Indian Wellington" and "the Indian Bonaparte," both sincere compliments from a European perspective, both invoking characters representing legend as well as history.

Other aspects of Tecumseh's life make his story especially amenable to mythologizing. For example, every heroic tale requires a worthy adversary for the protagonist. Tecumseh had on ongoing rivalry with one particular nemesis, William Henry Harrison, governor of the Indiana Territory and, during the War of 1812, Commander of the Army of the Northwest. Harrison stood for much of what Tecumseh fought against, such as the illegal purchase of American Indian land in the 1809 Treaty of Fort Wayne. Harrison also presented a major obstacle to Tecumseh's plans; his attack on Prophetstown, while Tecumseh was absent from his base of operations, yielded a costly but popular victory, one Harrison ultimately exploited as a campaign slogan and rode all the way to the U.S. presidency. According to legend, "Tecumseh's curse" explains President Harrison's untimely death after reaching the White House. The conflict between the adversaries, both real and imagined, is a lasting facet of Tecumseh's story.

Uncertainty also has added to the mystique of Tecumseh. Much of his life remains undocumented, from the exact details of his heritage to entire portions of his early years and later travels. As public and visible as

Tecumseh was as an international figure, many details about him remain elusive to historians. One example is the question of Tecumseh's remains. That Tecumseh died in the Battle of the Thames in Ontario on October 5, 1813, seems undisputed. Repeated attempts to solve the riddle of what happened to his body after his death remain inconclusive and ongoing, however, as interesting to modern readers and investigators as to his contemporaries. Like King Arthur—another European legend to whom Tecumseh has been repeatedly compared—Tecumseh's final resting place is a debated mystery that reflects as much about the myth as it does about the man.

Formed by an inextricable and contradictory tangle of fact and legend, the truth of Tecumseh is that no other nineteenth-century Native American, and perhaps no other American Indian of any time, is better known or more identifiable to mainstream audiences. His movement at the time reflected the highest achievement of a larger pan-tribal tradition and later informed other indigenous resistance and revitalization movements. Tecumseh's story is necessary for understanding the broader history of both Native America and North America.

TIMELINE: EVENTS IN THE LIFE OF TECUMSEH

c. 1768   Tecumseh is born in the Ohio Valley.

1774   October 10: Tecumseh's father is killed in the Battle of Point Pleasant.

1783   Joseph Brant rises as the leader of the Northwest Confederacy.

1789   Tecumseh goes with Cheeseekau to the home of the Chickamauga Cherokees.

1792   September 30: Shawnee Warrior (Cheeseekau) is killed at Buchanan's Station.

1794   August 20: The United States defeats the Northwest Confederacy in the Battle of Fallen Timbers.

1796   Tecumseh's son Paukeesaa is born, and Tecumseh sets up his first independent village with his followers.

1805   Lalawéthika becomes Tenskwatawa, the Prophet.

1808   The Prophet and Tecumseh found Prophetstown.

1809   The Treaty of Fort Wayne is signed.

1811   November 7: William Henry Harrison defeats the Prophetstown warriors at the Battle of Tippecanoe.

1812   June 18: The United States declares war on Great Britain.
August 16: William Hull surrenders Detroit to the British and American Indian armies.
October 13: Isaac Brock is killed in the Battle of Queenston Heights.

1813   January 22: The British and Native American forces defeat the British at the Battle of Frenchtown, and Native warriors commit the "River Raisin Massacre."
October 5: Tecumseh is killed in the Battle of the Thames (also known as the Battle of Moraviantown).

1814   December 24: The Treaty of Ghent ends the War of 1812.

Chapter 1

TECUMSEH'S WORLD

Many of the details of Tecumseh's birth, like much about his life and death, are surrounded by mystery, confused by contradictory accounts, and debated by scholars. Despite the uncertainty and controversy, however, a consensus has emerged about key elements of Tecumseh's early story. The remaining points of contention about Tecumseh are worth considering, as well, because those questions that are still argued today give us valuable information about Tecumseh and his times.

The tale begins on a day at some point between the years 1764 and 1771; many biographers find 1768 the likeliest date. A baby boy was born in a Shawnee town, perhaps Chillicothe or Kispoko Town, on the Scioto River, in the present-day state of Ohio. He was the fourth child in his family: his older siblings were his brother Cheeseekau ("The Sting"), his sister Tecumapease ("Flying over the Water," or "Wading Over"), and his brother Sauawaseekau ("Jumping Panther"). The baby was known as Tecumthé, but he later gained lasting international fame by a popular corruption of his name, Tecumseh. Four brothers followed, first Nehaas-eemoo, about whom very little is known, and then three triplets. One of the three died at birth. The other two were Kumskaukau ("A Cat That Flies in the Air," or perhaps "A Star Which Shoots in a Straight Line over Great Waters") and Laloeshiga ("A Panther with a Handsome Tail"). The latter soon earned the unflattering name Lalawéthika ("Noisy Rattle") from his family and neighbors. In adulthood, after his spiritual awakening, this brother chose the more dignified name of Tenskwatawa ("The Open Door"). His community chose a different nickname for him, however, and he became known simply as the Prophet.

The significance of Tecumseh's own name remains a subject of dispute. It might have been translated "Shooting Star" or "Blazing Comet." These meanings may give weight to the popular legend that Tecumseh's mother witnessed a good omen, a falling star or meteor shower, on the night her son was born. This story was widely spread during his lifetime, and it added credence to the idea that Tecumseh was destined for great deeds and recognized by the powers of the natural world. Scientists and historians have tried to correlate possible birth dates with reports of falling meteors and other astronomical events, but because of the quality of records and the sophistication of science at the time, the legend cannot be substantiated. Different interpretations of Tecumseh's name include "I Cross the Way" and "A Panther Crouching for His Prey." Both of these translations, as well as "Shooting Star" and "Blazing Comet," might support the theory that his name refers to his Shawnee clan affiliation. Shawnee children were born members of their fathers' clan; in Tecumseh's case, his clan, like his father's, was represented by a panther in the sky who crosses the heavens, stalking his prey among the stars. The names of some of his siblings appear to reference this clan symbol. This interpretation of Tecumseh's name, though less sensational than the meteor theory, matches not only common Shawnee practice at the time but also, it seems, the personal preferences of Tecumseh's family.

The backgrounds of Tecumseh's parents are also debated. His father, Pukeshinwau ("Something That Falls"), was a respected leader of the Kispoko Shawnees, one of five divisions of the Shawnee nation. It is possible that he helped to found, and was even chief of, Kispoko Town. According to some accounts, Pukeshinwau had an early, childless marriage to a Creek woman. Whether or not this was so, his wife Methoataaskee ("A Turtle Laying Her Eggs in the Sand") was the mother of his eight children. She was associated with the Pekowi division of the Shawnees and the turtle clan. Both husband and wife identified with and lived among the Shawnees, but neither Pukeshinwau's nor Methoataaskee's heritage is entirely clear. Some oral accounts during Tecumseh's time suggested that his mother was, in fact, Creek, although this assertion may have come from the fact that his parents had lived, along with the Tallapoosa Shawnees, among Creeks in present-day Alabama for a time before Tecumseh's birth. Some accounts speculate about partial Creek ancestry for Tecumseh's father. Others imply that Pukeshinwau was the son of a British trader—or perhaps even an English colonial governor, as Tecumseh's brother the Prophet asserted—and a Native American mother. It is possible that Pukeshinwau had an Anglo father; certainly interracial unions were not uncommon. Some evidence even supports this: in 1792, *The Knoxville*

Gazette described Tecumseh's brother Cheesekau as a "half-breed," and Tecumseh himself was described by those who knew him as "of an intermediate caste between a half white and a full-blooded Indian."[1]

Conflicting claims about Methoataaskee's background meant rather little; whether she was of Shawnee or Creek birth, an "original" or a "naturalized" Shawnee, was essentially irrelevant. Shawnee conceptions of ethnicity and citizenship were more fluid than those in the mainstream United States, and she and her children grew up fully embraced by and belonging to the Shawnee community. The mystery surrounding Pukeshinwau's heritage, however, might have enhanced his and later Tecumseh's reputation. For one thing, the idea of being the child of a powerful man such as a colonial governor would impart status, regardless of that man's race. Furthermore, if Pukeshinwau had proven too headstrong and unruly for a white father to handle and he had been returned to his American Indian mother because of this, it would be a source of pride for the Shawnees. Of course, to white audiences, Tecumseh's self-evident intelligence, sophistication, and good looks would be easier to accept if these admirable qualities could be attributed to non-Native ancestry.

In any case, his community recognized the infant Tecumseh as the Shawnee son of a respected leader. His inheritance included a long and distinguished cultural tradition, but it also included ongoing conflict. The exact origin of the Shawnee nation remains disputed. Some scholars have suggested that the Shawnees were the descendants of a prehistoric civilization known as the Fort Ancient culture, whose members inhabited the Ohio country (which included not only present-day Ohio but also portions of present-day West Virginia and Kentucky). Shawnee oral traditions held that the Shawnee were the first indigenous people created in North America, separate and different from others, but fellow Algonquin-speaking Native Americans apparently thought of the Shawnees as the southernmost siblings of the Great Lakes peoples. The Shawnee nation comprised five specific divisions (Mekoche, Hathawekela, Pekowi, Kispoko, and Chillicothe), and within these existed roughly a dozen clans. Before the eighteenth century, these Shawnee divisions scattered from their homeland, perhaps to flee the bloody mid-seventeenth-century wars (known as the French and Iroquois Wars, or the Beaver Wars, and which took place roughly between 1640 and 1698) between the Iroquois Confederacy and Algonquin-speaking Native Americans over the fur trade and its related territory. The Shawnees became too fragmented and separated to form a nation proper, unlike other native groups such as the Cherokees. Shawnee towns and villages grew up across the eastern half of the continent, as far northeast as Maryland, as far southeast as contemporary Florida, and as far southwest as present-day Alabama. Because Shawnees traveled far distances and traded and interacted with other peoples in the process, their language became spoken by many non-Shawnees. The fact that the Shawnee tongue became, in effect, an intertribal language later helped Tecumseh become an effective activist for pan-tribal unity.

Most Shawnees fled the seventeenth-century wars, but by the eighteenth century they proved willing to take up arms, first against Great Britain and its colonies and later against the United States. In the mid-eighteenth century, Shawnees fought with the French during the French and Indian War (1754–1763) and with other native nations in Pontiac's Rebellion (1763–1766), in both cases against the British. Some Shawnees had never left the Ohio River Valley in the first place; many others returned to resettle the area and reunite with their people, along with fellow Native American allies such as the Delawares and the Mingoes. Among those who returned to Ohio country in the mid-seventeenth century were Tecumseh's parents, who previously had been living in the south with fellow Shawnees among the Creeks. At some point during this time, Tecumseh's father, Pukeshinwau, added another member to his household: a white boy of three or four years of age, who had been abducted during the French and Indian Wars from Wheeling, West Virginia. How little Richard Sparks came to be under Pukeshinwau's protection— whether Pukeshinwau was his abductor or merely his adopter after his abduction—is unknown. Called Shawtunte by his Shawnee family, Sparks was raised as a foster son and became the particular playmate of Tecumseh's oldest brother, Cheeseekau, who was closest to his age.

With the British Proclamation of 1763, the Shawnees' Ohio homeland appeared to be safe from further colonial encroachment. This law created a line of demarcation between the British colonies in the east, which were open for settlement, and the land west of the Appalachian Mountains, which was off limits by law to colonists. Unfortunately for the Shawnees, this boundary did not remain unchanged for long. The Iroquois Confederacy, which was located in the region of New York, considered the Ohio territory theirs by right of conquest from the past wars, despite the fact that the Iroquois did not live there and the Shawnees and their neighbors did. Needless to say, the Shawnees did not recognize the Iroquois Confederacy's claim. Nevertheless, in 1768, the Iroquois agreed to the Treaty of Fort Stanwix, which extended British claims west into the valley, from the mouth of the Mohawk River in New York down the Ohio River to the mouth of the Tennessee River. White settlers began to move into areas where the Shawnees lived, farmed, and hunted—or, in the Shawnee perspective, to invade—even though no Shawnees had agreed to the treaty that opened the land to the colonists. As this upheaval began, probably in the very year of the Fort Stanwix Treaty, Tecumseh was born.

Tecumseh was brought into a world that was violent, insecure, and under continual threat. Following the Treaty of Fort Stanwix and the resulting influx of colonists, hostilities erupted between the Native Americans and settlers. Often the violence was unplanned and local, a series of small-scale strikes that ignited a chain reaction of retaliations and counterattacks. Shawnee leaders, in particular, sought to unify their neighbors against the British colonists. Although they hosted intertribal meetings and sent envoys in all directions to seek allies, even among the Iroquois, the Shawnees could not persuade other native nations to unify for a common cause. In 1774, Virginia's royal governor, Lord Dunmore, launched an invasion of the Ohio country in order to pacify the region. The different Shawnee divisions came together through their tribal council and decided to stand alone if necessary against the British forces. With only a few Mingo allies strengthening their numbers, the Shawnees went forth under the leadership of Chief Cornstalk. Among the warriors were Tecumseh's father, Pukeshinwau, and his eldest brother, Cheeseekau, who was barely a teenager.

On October 10, 1774, Cornstalk's forces met Dunmore's, which were led by Colonel Andrew Lewis, on the Ohio River near Point Pleasant, West Virginia. Badly outnumbered and outgunned, the Shawnees were defeated. The Battle of Point Pleasant, also known as the Battle of Kanawha, forced Cornstalk to concede the loss of Shawnee lands—effectively, the area that would become the state of Kentucky—through the Treaty of Camp Charlotte. The battle had a more immediate meaning to the young child Tecumseh: his father was killed during the day's fighting. Methoataaskee was left a widow in the late stages of pregnancy, with four of her own children as well as a foster son to protect. Pukeshinwau's triplet sons were born mere weeks after his death.

Tecumseh's childhood was marked by flight, danger, and uncertainty, as well as the conviction that the whites, or Long Knives, were the Shawnees' enemy. The end of Dunmore's War did not bring an end to individual acts of murder and reprisal on the Ohio frontier. Tecumseh's people were divided in spirit as well as geographically scattered: a split developed between the many Shawnees who refused to recognize the Treaty of Camp Charlotte or the loss of territory it represented and leaders such as Cornstalk, who accepted defeat and attempted to placate the British. Tecumseh's family was divided, as well. His father and one infant brother were dead. Furthermore, Cornstalk's strategy of cooperation with the British included returning all Shawnee prisoners of war from former conflicts; this meant giving up Shawtunte, or Richard Sparks, the white boy Pukeshinwau and Methoataaskee had fostered as their own for a dozen years. He was as unwilling to return to his people as Tecumseh's family was unwilling to let him go, but in the end they had very little choice. (Even as an adult who was aware of how he had been captured and forcibly taken from his home during the French and Indian War, Sparks continued to recall his adoptive Shawnee family, including young Tecumseh, with tremendous affection.) Losing Shawtunte meant that yet another constant in Tecumseh's young life disappeared. It is difficult to imagine how deeply the instability of his early years must have affected Tecumseh.

First Tecumseh lost members of his family, and then he lost his home. When the War of Independence broke out between the colonies and Great Britain, Cornstalk advised the Shawnees to remain neutral and avoid further bloodshed. This was not, he claimed, their fight. (Despite his pleas for peace, the chief nonetheless was murdered in 1777 by militiamen while unarmed, on a diplomatic trip to Fort Randolph.) Shawnee war leaders such as Blue Jacket, however, saw an opportunity to push the unwanted white settlers back over the Appalachian Mountains and so sided with the British against the colonials. Eventually, a majority of Shawnees followed Blue Jacket's lead and joined the British cause. Seeing the war drawing nearer, Methoataaskee took her children and moved west, where she hoped they would be safe from the conflict. She helped to build a new town, named Pekowi, on the northwestern bank of the Mad River, just west of present-day Springfield, Ohio. Other communities grew up nearby, including Shawnee, Mingo, and Delaware towns. The war leader Blackfish lived in the nearby town of Old Chillicothe. According to some reports, he apparently served as a foster father to Tecumseh and his siblings for a short while until he, too, was taken from them by violence.

Methoataaske's hope of peace in the west was short-lived. The war moved west with the migrating Shawnees. Wooden stockades appeared along with British agents, French Canadian traders, and scouts of all kinds. Warriors from local allies such as the Mingoes and Delawares and more distant Great Lakes nations such as the Potawatomis and Wyandots passed through on their way to and from the fighting. The conflict came uncomfortably close to Tecumseh on the night of May 29, 1779. Three hundred Kentuckians launched a surprise attack against the town of Old Chillicothe in retaliation for Shawnee support of the British. Warriors from Pekowi rode to the town's defense. Several Shawnees were killed, including the war leader Blackfish. After that, it was only a matter of time before Methoataaske would be forced to move her family yet again.

Tecumseh must have grown accustomed to seeing war parties come and go with the wounded and dead. Sometimes these groups of warriors brought with them prisoners of war, who were considered the property of their individual captors, to be either adopted and loved or tortured and killed. A large force of British and Native American troops, including Shawnees, attacked Kentucky the year after the attack on Old Chillicothe. In this raid, approximately 350 captives were taken, including a white boy named Stephen Ruddell, who was Tecumseh's age. Dubbed Sinnamatha, or "Big Fish," he became part of the Shawnee community and a lifelong friend of Tecumseh. The Shawnee attack responsible for bringing Stephen Ruddell yielded dire consequences, however. In August 1780, while many Shawnee warriors were away fighting in Detroit, one thousand colonial troops from Kentucky burned Old Chillicothe to ashes. The attack gave the Shawnees of Pekowi and Kispoko Town time to flee before their communities met similar fates. Tecumseh probably hid on the bluffs behind his home with his mother and younger siblings and watched as his home was destroyed.

Once again, the Shawnees relocated, this time to the northwest. Those who were not away fighting the war on other fronts founded new settlements along the banks of the Great Miami and Mad Rivers. And, once again, the Kentuckians struck. In 1782, a Kentucky force approximately one thousand strong hit the new settlements and forced another Shawnee retreat along the rivers. During these years of constant threat and upheaval, Tecumseh drew especially close to two of his siblings, who became perhaps the most influential figures in his childhood. One was his sister, Tecumapease, who served as his primary caretaker and source of stability. Sometime during these years she also married a warrior named Wahsikegaboe ("Stands Firm"), who became a leader in his own right and, like Tecumapease, an important supporter of Tecumseh's movement. Tecumseh remained devoted and close to his sister throughout his life. The other influence was his eldest brother, Cheeseekau, who soon earned the name Pepquannake ("Gun Shot") as a warrior. He had faced his first battle in Dunmore's War, in which their father was slain; although he continued to fight, he also took Pukeshinwau's place within the family, instructing Tecumseh in hunting, fighting, and developing the character of an honorable Shawnee man. Tecumseh's legendary adherence to a strict moral code had its root, most likely, in Cheeseekau's early, conscientious instruction. It seems clear that Tecumseh sought to follow in his eldest brother's footsteps as a warrior and a man. Both Tecumapease and Cheeseekau undoubtedly helped Tecumseh survive, emotionally and intellectually as well as physically, a childhood that was nothing short of traumatic. His friends, acquaintances, biographers, and even enemies would express surprise at the consistent sense of justice, compassion, energy, and purpose that Tecumseh possessed, despite the difficulties of his earliest years.

Eventually, the final victory by the revolutionaries in 1783 meant defeat not only for the British but also for the Shawnees. The end of the war found the Shawnees and their allies, the Mingoes and the Delawares, weakened and far-flung, their warriors now outnumbered by armed white men in the Kentucky region. The fighting, however, was far from over.

NOTE

1. Quoted in John Sudgen, *Tecumseh: A Life* (New York: Henry Holt, 1997), p. 15.

Chapter 2

COMING OF AGE

The next few years proved to be a crucial time for Tecumseh. The Shawnee nation faced new crises. Following his brother Cheeseekau, Tecumseh began to play an active role in the story of his people and to develop a reputation among them. Moreover, as the new United States moved into the Northwest Territory, Native American bids for pan-tribal unity laid the foundation for what later would become Tecumseh's life's work.

No information survives about when Tecumseh underwent the traditional Shawnee rite of passage known as the vision quest, but we can assume it took place sometime during the Revolutionary War period, as Tecumseh entered puberty. Cheeseekau probably prepared his younger brother and oversaw the ritual. The custom was generations old. Through the solitude, fasting, and prayer of the vision quest, young Shawnees sought the identity of their guardian spirits. Each individual was believed to have a unique spirit guide—beyond the various spirits considered to be common to all clan members or to all Shawnees—who served as both a personal protector and a source of power. Tecumseh would have blackened his face, to symbolize his fast, and retreated to a solitary place to reflect and pray. Perhaps he undertook the quest in a series of stages, each with a longer fast. At the end of the experience, he would have emerged with a vision of his personal spirit guide, most likely in animal form. He would have kept this knowledge as a sacred secret throughout his life and created a medicine bag to carry items that helped him remember and reflect upon his guardian spirit. Upon his return from this ritual, Tecumseh would have been seen by his community as well on his way to manhood.

Various stories emerge about Tecumseh's teen years from accounts given by friends, relatives, and acquaintances. Some of these reports were made long after the fact, but yet they are repeated by biographers to this day. It is difficult, if not impossible, to prove or disprove these tales or to separate fully the legends that surrounded the older Tecumseh—and perhaps affected the memories of those who remembered him—from the reality of his adolescence. In fact, even the original sources of some of these tales are unclear. This uncertainty does not necessarily render these tales useless to students of Tecumseh, however, because these stories inform the myth of Tecumseh, even if they do not accurately portray the facts of his life. There is no doubt that these stories were often retold and that they are influential for contemporary and later historical understandings of the man.

One such tale suggests that the young Tecumseh was so serious about his chosen path that he shunned relationships with women in order to focus with singleminded intensity on growing into and living up to the role of a Shawnee warrior. This was particularly significant because he was said to have had more than his share of female admirers. Tecumseh was evidently unusually handsome even at a young age; later reports, even including official U.S. accounts, consistently mention his impressive and noble physical appearance. Some variations of the story imply that he went so far as to avoid mixed-gender hunting parties for a long time, so no women would have the opportunity to pursue him in a smaller group or a more intimate setting. Perhaps there is some truth to the idea that he followed his goals to the exclusion of more personal and domestic pleasures such as romance. Records indicate that the adult Tecumseh failed to have a lasting and successful relationship with a woman. Stories of earlier self-denial speak to the sense of purpose and commitment that others found unusual and admirable in Tecumseh.

Another story offers a different, perhaps less complimentary explanation of Tecumseh's desire to prove himself as a warrior. Accounts disagree. Some place the date as early as 1782, others as late as 1786; some identify the adversaries as Kentuckian troops bent on attack, others as traders and settlers peacefully on their way to Kentucky. The general story, however, remains the same. Tecumseh followed his brother Cheeseekau and a war party to the Mad River, which was often navigated by flatboats carrying munitions, supplies, and livestock, as well as U.S. soldiers and civilians. The party intended to harass the river traffic, hoping to dissuade others from undertaking similar trips. Close, violent fighting ensued. Cheeseekau sustained a minor wound during the battle. Tecumseh, new to such violence, panicked and ran. Although he later returned to the scene of the fighting and received forgiveness for abandoning the war party, the shame of his failure overcame him. He was doubly motivated to prove his courage and abilities. Tecumseh's later prowess as a warrior and a leader of men in battle, then, had its root in an early, bitter experience, according to the tale. This story certainly humanizes Tecumseh and makes his accomplishments all the more impressive because of his fallibility. This account might also have been used in instructing and encouraging young warriors, since heroic figures like the great Tecumseh made mistakes, too, and proved that they could be overcome.

A third tale also comments on Tecumseh's ability to learn from a mistake and make amends for it, while also reflecting well on his skills as a hunter. Sometime after the end of the U.S. War of Independence, so the story goes, Tecumseh went hunting. U.S. forces were known to be advancing on the area, and the war chief in authority had instructed everyone to give these troops a wide berth and stay out of their path. Tecumseh found several buffaloes watering at a stream; despite the fact that he knew the area lay directly on the route the white soldiers were following, he killed the buffaloes and returned to the community with his bounty. The war chief was furious at Tecumseh's disobedience and struck him. The next day, Tecumseh went with a friend to hunt in a different direction. They came upon buffaloes running in a herd. Both climbed into a tree and took aim. Tecumseh's friend killed one buffalo as it ran beneath him; using only his bow and arrows, Tecumseh killed sixteen. He returned to his community redeemed by the generous fruits of his hunt, and he even received a gun as a reward for his skills and efforts. Although this tale of Tecumseh's prowess and perseverance cannot be accepted wholeheartedly as fact, the story and its implications of Tecumseh's unique abilities even at a young age have become part of Tecumseh's legend through numerous retellings.

While Tecumseh was growing up—observing the Shawnee rites of passage, learning to hunt and fight—the leaders of the fledgling United States were making choices about how to deal with the American Indians of the Northwest. The situation was complicated by the fact that many of these natives had fought against the colonies during the War of Independence. An opportunity existed for peace between the new country and the native nations. Instead, the United States pursued an aggressive policy of expansionism that led to a new war. After the Treaty of Paris ended hostilities between the United States and its mother country in 1783, British policy in North America reflected little concern for former allies such as the Shawnees. Encouraged, U.S. leaders decided to annex the lands that lay north of the Ohio River and east of the Great Miami—in short, the land that remained to the Shawnees, Mingoes, and Delawares after the

Treaty of Fort Stanwix. When news of these U.S. plans reached Native Americans in and around the Ohio Valley, the outcry was immediate.

Not only the Shawnees, Mingoes, and Delawares felt threatened; others believed this intended annexation would be the first of many. Ironically, it was the Iroquois Confederacy—the same group that had surrendered Shawnee land in the Treaty of Fort Stanwix—that organized an inter-tribal conference in 1783 to discuss the situation. Representatives of the Iroquois nations attended this meeting at Lower Sandusky near Lake Erie, as did leaders from many other groups, from the Shawnees and Dela-wares and Potawatomis to the Wyandots and Creeks and Cherokees. A pan-tribal movement took shape, one that would live more than a decade and directly inspire Tecumseh's own plan for American Indian resistance. The Mohawk leader Thayendanegea, better known as Joseph Brant, be-came the leader and spokesman for the Northwest Confederacy organized by the conference attendees.

The ideas that undergirded the confederacy were twofold. First, Ameri-can Indian nations had to support one another militarily in the face of U.S. westward expansion; an attack on one group was a threat to all. Sec-ond, and even more important, these groups could not allow the United States to divide them and to use them against one another at the negoti-ating table. Experience with the colonies had proved that members of one tribe might sell or surrender lands to which they had no traditional claim. The Shawnees knew this firsthand. As insurance against any further such illegitimate agreements, all future land sales required the approval of the combined representatives of all of the native nations. In short, only the confederacy could ratify land sales. By treating the lands as if they were held in common by the native nations, requiring the consent of all to sell, the confederacy made certain that the United States would not be able to alienate any specific nation from its specific territory. The point of both ideas, military and diplomatic, was to unify in order to resist U.S. encroachment. As Joseph Brant later said to the Commissioners of the United States, "The people you see here are sent to represent the Indian nations who own the lands north of the Ohio as their common property, and who are all of one mind—one heart."[1]

The very thing the Northwest Confederacy hoped to avoid, however, almost immediately came to pass—three times. The three agreements to-gether became known as the Conquest Treaties. The first was negotiated, once again, at Fort Stanwix with the Iroquois (in the notable absence of Joseph Brant). This time, the United States claimed the right of conquest, demanding that the Iroquois surrender any surviving claims to the Ohio country. To the indignation of their native allies, they did. The 1785 Treaty of Fort McIntosh caused even greater outrage. U.S. representatives made an agreement in which members of the Wyandot, Delaware, Ojibwe, and Ottawa nations ceded large portions of southern and eastern Ohio country; while fully protecting their own homes, they gave away portions of the Shawnee homeland. The Shawnee war chief Captain Johnny summed up the Shawnee response when he rebuked those who had signed the treaty and reminded them of the confederacy: "All nations of us of one color were there and agreed as one man...one or two nations going to our brothers' council fire cannot do anything without the whole there present."[2]

U.S. agents used more force than diplomacy on the Shawnees in 1786. Calling for them to attend a meeting at the mouth of the Great Miami, U.S. forces built a stockade there named Fort Finney, a clear show of strength and permanent presence. When the elderly civil chief Moluntha and his people explained that they could not negotiate without the rest of the Shawnees and all representatives of the Northwest Confederacy in attendance, the federal commissioners threatened them with immediate war. Under duress, the Shawnees present—a minority of the nation— agreed to U.S. terms. The combined Conquest Treaties effectively meant that the Shawnees had lost their Ohio homeland. The first two agreements had caused fury among the Shawnees. The last meant bloodshed.

The leaders of Shawnee nation immediately denounced all three of the treaties and began to organize for war against the United States. Neighboring Mingoes, Delawares, and Cherokees followed their lead, as well. Calls went to the west, to the native nations of the Wabash River Valley, to join the Shawnees and lend their support. The argument for unity was compelling: if those in the Wabash chose not to fight now, they would be the next targets of the United States. U.S. forces, concerned over the rapid Shawnee mobilization, seemed to make the Shawnees' case for them; in a preemptive strike, militia troops led by Benjamin Logan attacked the Shawnee nation. His choice of targets could not possibly have been worse; the town of Mackachack was the home of the aged chief Moluntha, who had agreed to the Fort Finney treaty and continued to counsel peace to anyone who would listen. The force attacked while most able-bodied Shawnee men were hunting. Some of the remaining Shawnees attempted to raise the U.S. flag in Mackachack as a show of goodwill, but all were either killed or taken prisoner. Moluntha surrendered peacefully. While being held in custody and questioned by Colonel Hugh McCrary, the old Shawnee chief was killed—not unlike Shawnee Chief Cornstalk, who had been murdered while he, too, was an unarmed prisoner. Before they retreated, Logan's soldiers laid waste to six Shawnee villages, including Tecumseh's hometown.

The raids were repaid with nine years of warfare between the Northwest Confederacy and the United States for the Northwest Territory. They also marked an end to whatever had remained of Tecumseh's childhood. By this time his brother Cheeseekau had achieved the status of a respected minor war leader commanding his own group of warriors. Tecumseh joined them. The first tasks for the Shawnees were by now familiar ones: retreat, regroup, rebuild. They established new towns at the intersection of the St. Marys and St. Joseph Rivers, which formed the head of the Maumee River, near the present-day city of Fort Wayne, Indiana. These communities included Shawnees, Miamis, and Delawares, all of whom denied the legitimacy of the recent U.S. actions toward their nations and neighbors.

They were not alone. Joseph Brant breathed new life into the wounded confederacy and called a meeting at the Wyandot town of Brownstone, which sat at the mouth of the Detroit River. There the confederacy declared all three Conquest Treaties null and void. As before, the members called on the United States to negotiate with the confederacy as a whole if its leaders wished to make legitimate treaties that the Native Americans would respect as legally binding. The U.S. response was not altogether promising. The Northwest Ordinance, passed by the Continental Congress in July 1787, set up an administration system for the Northwest Territory and rules by which the areas within it could become states. (This area later became the states of Ohio, Indiana, Illinois, Michigan, and Wisconsin and formed a portion of the state of Minnesota.) The governor of the new Northwest Territory, Arthur St. Clair, was given authority to buy the land—that is, pay for the land—already taken by the Conquest Treaties. Returning the lands, or renegotiating the boundaries of the ceded areas, was not an option.

During this time, Cheeseekau and his warriors, including Tecumseh, sought to worry and harass U.S. forces and white settlers in every possible way. They targeted the flatboats that brought settlers, livestock, and supplies down the Ohio River to Kentucky. One particular attack, which took place in 1788, reflected the maturing Tecumseh's character in terms of both combat and conscience. Cheeseekau and a mixed force of Shawnees, Cherokees, Mingoes, and so-called white Indians, or former Kentucky captives who had assimilated into native culture, raided three flatboats. The crews resisted, and there was fierce, close fighting. Tecumseh did not falter; in fact, he proved himself more than equal to the other warriors. Stephen Rudell, Tecumseh's friend, recalled that this was "the first engagement in which he particularly distinguished himself," and his courage "even left in the background some of the oldest and bravest warriors."[3]

The war party killed some of the crew and passengers during the guerrilla-style hits. They took others as their prisoners to be ransomed, sold, adopted, or killed later. A number survived and eventually returned to their homes, but one unfortunate captive was burned alive after the raid. Although this practice of torture and execution was traditional—the "owner" of the prisoner could choose his or her fate—Tecumseh showed tremendous disgust at the burning. He thought such actions were cruel and inhumane, not to mention cowardly. He did not express his feelings against the burning until after it was completed, but witnessing the murder obviously made a tremendous impact on Tecumseh. He interceded for other prisoners throughout his career and forbade his followers to torture or execute their helpless captives. This early raid reflected two sides of Tecumseh that would become his trademarks as he grew older: the dangerous, fearless warrior, dedicated to winning on the battlefield, and the merciful, civilized man, devoted to justice. Even as a youth, he showed the desire not only to fulfill the warrior's code but to go a step farther and fulfill his own strict standard of personal honor. As one of his earliest biographers, Benjamin Drake, wrote in 1841, "He was then but a boy, yet he had the independence to attack a cherished custom of his tribe, and the power of argument to convince them, against all their preconceived notions of right and the rules of warfare, that the custom [of burning prisoners alive] should be abolished. That this effort...was the result of a humane disposition, and a right sense of justice, is abundantly shown by his conduct toward prisoners in after life."[4]

Despite successes such as the capture of the flatboats, Cheeseekau apparently grew dissatisfied conducting small-scale raids with his war party while new settlers and troops continued to move into the region. He considered leaving the area altogether and seeking a place far removed from the threat of U.S. encroachment. A trader known to the Shawnees, Louis Lorimier, had relocated earlier to Spanish territory over the Mississippi River, in present-day Missouri. He now invited the Shawnees and their neighbors to join him. Spain welcomed Native settlers. The Spanish were not completely altruistic in offering their protection to the dispossessed nations, however; they perceived themselves to be in a precarious position and needed people to serve as a buffer population between the Osages in the west, who always seemed to be fighting, and the United States in the east, which always seemed to be expanding. The opportunity sounded ideal to Cheeseekau. In 1788, Cheeseekau set off for the Spanish territory with his warriors, including Tecumseh, and his younger twin brothers, Lalawéthika and Kumskaukau.

The trip proved especially fateful for Tecumseh. While hunting for buffaloes en route to Spanish territory, Tecumseh suffered a fall from his horse. His thighbone shattered so badly it could not be set effectively. The party halted for the winter to stay with the wounded young man. It seemed that, just as he was becoming a warrior and hunter and adult, Tecumseh might be crippled for life, unable to follow his brother or his intended path of life. When spring came, Cheeseekau urged Tecumseh to remain camped with some of the party in order to continue to recuperate, while he took the rest of the band to settle over the Mississippi. Tecumseh refused, however, and made the arduous journey with the help of crutches. The injury took a long time to heal, and he was left with a scar and a permanent limp, but it could have been far worse. Accounts offer an interesting insight into Tecumseh's psyche: while he was bedridden during the long winter months, he reportedly sank into a desperate, possibly life-threatening depression, but when the spring came and he could take action, despite the discomfort and difficulty of continuing on, he met the challenge with energy and resolve.

Tecumseh received a second blow when, by stubborn determination, he finally made his painful way to the end of his journey. The American Indians were not the only settlers the Spaniards had invited to relocate in their territory. The Spanish had given another former trader the assignment of wooing whites from the United States to build communities in the area. Cheeseekau and his band had left their home to seek a place outside of the reach of U.S. settlers, only to find that those same settlers had reached it before them. The Shawnees did not contemplate staying. They turned and left. If they could not find peace in Spanish territory, Cheeseekau determined, he and his party would find war in the land claimed by the United States. They crossed the Mississippi River once more and headed southeast, for the home of the very fiercest indigenous opposition to the United States: the mountain strongholds of the Chickamauga Cherokees.

NOTES

1. Quoted in C. F. Klinck, ed., *Tecumseh: Fact and Fiction in Early Records* (Ottawa: Tecumseh Press, 1978), p. 10.

2. Quoted in John Sudgen, *Tecumseh: A Life* (New York: Henry Holt, 1997), p. 45.

3. Ibid., p. 51.

4. Quoted in Klinck, *Tecumseh:Fact and Fiction in Early Records*, p. 23.

Chapter 3

FROM FOLLOWER TO LEADER

Over the next several years, Tecumseh learned a great deal about leadership both from his brother and from a new role model, the Cherokee war leader Dragging Canoe. He also faced two critical turning points in his life that transformed him from a warrior, the follower of his brother Cheeseekau, into a leader: he had his first experience directing a war party on his own, over a great distance during a dangerous time, and he experienced a tragic loss that cemented his position as a Shawnee leader in his own right. As Tecumseh assumed his new role of leader, external hostilities and internal disharmony threatened all that he held dear and brought to the forefront some of the challenges to which he would devote the rest of his adult life.

After their disappointment in the Spanish territory across the Mississippi, Cheeseekau and his band chose to visit the Chickamauga Cherokees, a group who had a long-standing relationship with the Shawnees. The Chickamaugas were not a separate internal division of the Cherokee nation; they earned their name from U.S. officials who used it to denote the followers of the bold and uncompromising Cherokee war chief Dragging Canoe. The Cherokee nation was located to the southeast of the Shawnees, concentrated in present-day Georgia, North and South Carolina, and Tennessee. The miles had not kept a distance between the Cherokee and Shawnee peoples, however. At the request of the Shawnee leader Cornstalk, Dragging Canoe had fought against the "Long Knives" who had settled west of the Appalachians and who threatened the native nations of the Ohio Valley. Because of this support of his allies to the north, Dragging Canoe and his Cherokees had faced serious reprisals from colonial forces. He eventually separated from the Cherokee nation proper and withdrew with his followers to the area that is now Chattanooga, Tennessee. There they established the town of Chickamauga and various other settlements, carefully concealed and protected in the mountains and valleys.

While other Cherokee leaders urged caution and sought peace, Dragging Canoe consistently followed a path of military resistance against the whites. He gained additional supporters as his fellow Cherokees learned that signing official compacts with colonial governments did little or nothing to protect them from independent attacks and incursions by the settlers of those colonies. Since diplomatic agreements offered no promise of safety, increasing numbers of Cherokees and their native neighbors became sympathetic to the continual state of war that Dragging Canoe recognized between his people and the Anglos. Dragging Canoe denied the validity of all the treaties with the British colonies and later the United States. He sought to strike in any way he could at the whites, whom he saw as invaders.

The tactics of guerrilla warfare that Dragging Canoe practiced relied on surprise, stealth, and speed. He and his warriors targeted the traffic—official and civilian—on major waterways such as the Watauga, Holston, Nolichucky, Cumberland, and Tennessee Rivers. They also attacked unwary travelers on the primary trails to the west, including the Cumberland Trail, the Nickajack Trail, and the Natchez Trace, among others. In such raids, the warriors could deal a double blow to their victims, either killing or capturing the people and also taking possession of the goods and supplies they often moved along such major routes. From their base in Chickamauga, Dragging Canoe's forces spread in all directions to strike in Virginia, Georgia, North and South Carolina, Kentucky territory, and the Ohio country.

Dragging Canoe was something of a living legend by the time Tecumseh met him. He was notorious not only for his fierce war making but also for his stubborn resilience in the face of repeated setbacks. He had suffered many. In 1779, Virginians attacked and devastated the towns Dragging Canoe and his people had built. Word of the destruction reached the Shawnees, and they sent a delegation to Chickamauga to represent the friendship between their two peoples. The groups exchanged forces in order to strengthen their alliance; Cherokee warriors returned to Ohio with the Shawnee delegation, and Shawnee warriors remained in Chickamauga to help Dragging Canoe rebuild his community—and, of course, continue the raids against the colonists.

In 1782, the Chickamauga towns once more were destroyed. Dragging Canoe and his people relocated westward, into the more defensible hills bordered by the Tennessee River and Lookout Mountain (at the juncture of present-day Georgia, Tennessee, and Alabama). With the permission of the Muskogees, who owned this region, the Cherokees established towns in this secluded area and embraced an ever-growing loose confederation of peoples, from Cherokees and Shawnees and other Native Americans to runaway slaves and sympathetic Anglo traders of various nationalities. Dragging Canoe tried to unify the disparate groups who supported resistance; he sent warriors to the Shawnees, Choctaws, and Delawares and met with the Cherokees, Muskogees, Chickasaws, and Choctaws in a general council. After the colonies won the War of Independence, however, the Cherokees' story must have seemed all too familiar to the Shawnees. Cession treaties were made, arguably under duress, such as the 1785 Treaty of Hopewell, which Dragging Canoe neither signed nor supported. Two respected chiefs, Old Tassel and Abraham, were murdered by U.S. forces while under a flag of truce. The transition of the colonies into states made the situation even worse for the Cherokees, it seemed.

The Chickamauga Cherokees continued to resist U.S. expansion despite—or because of—these developments. Militia forces attacked Dragging Canoe's people in their new location, but the Chickamaugas thoroughly repelled the assaults. The war chief proved capable of rebuilding time and again, successful in defending his new mountain home, determined to offer constant military resistance to the United States, and hopeful of creating an alliance of many groups devoted to this purpose. At this point, Cheeseekau and his Shawnee party joined him in his mountain stronghold. Dragging Canoe's example no doubt greatly influenced young Tecumseh.

Cheeseekau and his Shawnee band based their guerrilla operations in the central Chickamauga town of Running Water. From this position, they made attacks on their own and also participated in raids with their Chickamauga allies. One example illustrates the tension and distrust that typified U.S.-Native contact during this time. Some Chickamaugas encountered a U.S. officer with a detachment of soldiers on the Tennessee River. His name was Major John Doughty, and he claimed he was on a mission of peace, to encourage trade and friendly relations. (This was correct; he bore a message directly from President George Washington, in fact.) The Native Americans were suspicious of him, however. They pondered his story. It seemed suspicious that he brought no goods, if in fact he wished to promote trade. It likewise seemed suspicious that he brought soldiers, if in fact he desired peace. After recent attacks on the Chickamauga settlements, some feared that the troops intended to build a fort on American Indian land and then send reinforcements to threaten the

Chickamaugas and their neighbors. A team of Cherokees, Shawnees, and Creeks formed to attack Doughty and his men. Cheeseekau led them—a fact that reflects his standing in the community—and it is probable that Tecumseh followed. They surrounded Doughty on his barge in the river, killing or wounding nine of his fifteen men. He barely escaped and never delivered his message from Washington.

Tecumseh certainly took part in many similar raids and attacks. Many sources suggest that he also took a Cherokee wife, or at least a lover, early in his time in Dragging Canoe's settlement. Although her name is lost to record, multiple reports confirm that she and Tecumseh had a daughter together; this daughter apparently relocated with other Cherokees voluntarily to Arkansas country, where she was still living in 1825. Her Cherokee children were commonly recognized throughout the region as Tecumseh's grandchildren. It would not have been unusual for Tecumseh and his love to forgo traditional wedding rites, since at that time it was becoming increasingly common for couples to live together and even raise families without benefit of marriage. (Ironically, this prevalent circumventing of traditional ceremonies and institutions would be criticized by Tecumseh's brother the Prophet during his religious revitalization movement.) Even if they had wed, both Shawnee and Cherokee traditions included rather simple steps for dissolving marriage unions without attributing fault to either party. Although their relationship did not endure, accounts by Tecumseh's friends indicate that this was perhaps the happiest and most long-lived of Tecumseh's few romantic liaisons.

After two years among the Chickamaugas, Tecumseh agreed to lead part of the Shawnee group back to the Ohio Valley. This trip in the summer of 1791 was his first real foray into independent leadership, since Cheeseekau remained with Dragging Canoe's people. The Northwest Confederacy was in trouble, and Tecumseh planned to assist however he could before rejoining his older brother in the south. While he and Cheeseekau were with Dragging Canoe, the Mohawk leader Joseph Brant had tried to reform and reinvigorate a confederacy weakened by the Conquest Treaties and their aftermath. Despite Brant's efforts, however, members of the native nations proved unable to work together. Boycotts, walkouts, and land cessions resulted from Native attempts to negotiate collectively with U.S. officials.

When Brant failed to get the Native Americans to cooperate, the Shawnees, who had relocated to towns along the Maumee River, tried to reforge the broken alliances of the confederacy themselves. U.S. troops attacked them in 1790, and the Shawnees united with Miamis, Delawares,

Mingoes, and Cherokees to defeat them. The clear victory they won drew attention and seemed to suggest that the spirit of pan-tribal unity was not lost. Any rebirth of the confederacy, however, meant that another attack by the Long Knives of the United States was imminent. Calls went out for warriors to take part in the impending conflict. Tecumseh and some of Cheeseekau's other followers—including their two brothers—responded.

The watershed moment of this conflict occurred on November 4, 1791, when Governor Arthur St. Clair ordered his army to march against the Maumee towns. A greatly outnumbered Native force, led by Blue Jacket, Little Turtle, and Buckongahelas, opposed the white soldiers. Tecumseh was leading a band of scouts who were spying on enemy troop movements at some distance from the fighting, and he could not reach the field in time to take part in the battle. Nevertheless, the Native American force turned back the U.S. troops and cost them more than one thousand casualties. The Shawnees and their allies were, for a while at least, safe. The overwhelming victory inspired confidence; to the most militant American Indians, it seemed possible that U.S. expansion west might be not only halted but even reversed, until no permanent U.S. settlements remained north of the Ohio River.

Although he missed fighting in this key battle, Tecumseh found opportunities to distinguish himself. Early in 1792, for example, he led a hunting party along the Little Miami River. His band had no reason to expect hostilities while searching for food. One night after dark, however, a party of Kentuckians came upon Tecumseh's camp, surrounded it, and attacked. They opened fire without warning on the sleeping tents of the hunters. The situation was a recipe for slaughter. Although he was taken by surprise, Tecumseh quickly and coolly rallied the other hunters and developed a strategy. At Tecumseh's instruction, the hunters did not simply defend themselves; they counterattacked, charging against the Kentuckians. The Native Americans were outnumbered approximately three to one, and yet, as Tecumseh had expected, their quick rally and response convinced the Kentuckians that their number was far larger. The attackers withdrew in a scattered retreat. The hunters praised Tecumseh's bold leadership, while the surviving Kentuckians, perhaps still in confusion or simply to protect themselves from embarrassment, later claimed to have met a military force of a hundred men or more, rather than a hunting party of seven or eight. Tecumseh's reputation for daring and cleverness grew.

To the south, Cheeseekau also was making a name for himself. The famed Dragging Canoe had died and was succeeded by the war chief John Watts, and the violence in the region continued to swell. Cheeseekau fought with his allies like a man possessed; to the Shawnees, he was Pepquannake ("Gun Shot"); to his Chickamauga allies and U.S. foes, he was simply Shawnee Warrior. Fueled by anger and frustration, he participated in a number of bloody raids. According to widespread rumor, he had killed three hundred men by this time and had voiced his desire to double this number. In September 1792, it seemed he would get his chance. In council, the Chickamaugas determined to undertake a new and ambitious military campaign: a strike against the burgeoning town of Nashville on the Cumberland River. Cheeseekau spoke openly for this act of war and pledged his followers, including roughly thirty warriors, to the effort. Tecumseh and those who had gone with him to Ohio returned to join Cheeseekau in the campaign. Together they formed part of a larger force led by John Watts himself.

The Shawnees should have been pleased by this reunion and excited about their new plan of action, but instead the party was wary and uneasy. Cheeseekau had told his brother and the other warriors that he had received a premonition of his own death. Whether he had experienced a dream or vision is unclear, but Shawnees placed great weight on such forewarnings, and Cheeseekau apparently took it very seriously. The venture seemed doomed before it had begun. Despite the concern of his comrades, though, Cheeseekau could not be persuaded to change his plans. He went forward with the rest of the warriors toward Nashville. On the morning of September 30, 1792, the multitribal Chickamauga force encountered and killed two scouts from Nashville. By that evening, the Native Americans reached Buchanan's Station, a small fort four miles south of the town. U.S. Major John Buchanan was in charge of the fortification and its men, who numbered approximately fifteen.

Late that night or very early the following morning, John Watts and his warriors attacked the fort. The Cherokees, Creeks, and Shawnees seized the animals and supplies outside the walls of Buchanan's Station, but they could not seem to make headway against its fortifications. Although they were well armed and vastly outnumbered the fort's staff, the Chickamaugas could not even wound, much less kill, the soldiers or civilians within the structure. After repeated attempts to take Buchanan's Station, the warriors abandoned the failed attack. The engagement had yielded disastrous results. Watts himself was badly wounded. Two of the group's leaders, Chiachattalley (or Chiachattalla) and Little Owl, the brother of Dragging Canoe, lay dead.

For Tecumseh, the night marked a personal tragedy; one of the first volleys shot from the fort had struck Cheeseekau in the forehead, killing him instantly. Tecumseh took the body of his brother, his leader, the man who had been a father figure to him throughout his life, and gave him a Shawnee burial. In one blow, Tecumseh inherited the respected mantle of his war hero father and the leadership role of his notorious warrior brother. The band of Shawnees amid the Chickamauga force looked to him for direction. He swore he would avenge Cheeseekau's death before returning to the Ohio Valley.

Although Tecumseh had private reasons for wishing to fight the U.S. military and settlers in the west—reasons such as the deaths of his brother and father, the destruction of his home, the dispossession of his people— he did not go to battle with the same consuming anger that Cheeseekau had shown in his final days. Instead, Tecumseh continued to balance his warrior aggression with his humanitarian conscience and his larger sense of purpose, his desire for Native unity. For a time after the Buchanan's Station defeat, he continued making small raids against various targets with Chickamaugas and their allies. Once, while traveling with a war party made up of Cherokees, Creeks, and Shawnees and led by Middle Striker, Tecumseh and his fellow warriors ambushed Captain Samuel Handley and his militia force who were heading west from Knoxville. The surprise attack overwhelmed the troops, most of whom fled. A few were killed, and Captain Handley was taken prisoner. While a captive, Handley suffered quite enough to make an example and warning of his experience to other U.S. officers, although his ordeal was caused as much by the fever he contracted as by the mistreatment he suffered at the hands of his captors. Months later, upon his release, he told a harrowing story of how some of the American Indians had prepared to burn him alive. According to Handley, a warrior who had taken part in his original cap- ture, a minor war leader, had spoken eloquently on his behalf, saving him from a terrible death. Considering Tecumseh's outspoken opposition to the torture and execution of prisoners, many identified Handley's savior as Tecumseh.

Tecumseh took part for some time in the raids and battles of the Chick- amaugas, but, at last, believing Cheeseekau properly avenged and eager to take part in the life of the revived Northwest Confederacy, he led his Shawnees back to the Ohio country. While seeking food on the journey, his hunting party was attacked by superior numbers, possibly led by famed scout and trader Robert McClellan. Tecumseh, though surprised, reacted with the same speed and control that he had shown the previous spring in similar circumstances. With little time to plan or communicate, he organized his men and led a charge against his foes. His astonished at- tackers fled so quickly that they even left behind some of their supplies, which the members of Tecumseh's party gladly salvaged. By this time

Tecumseh had established a pattern of leaving any spoils of battle to his warriors, a practice that gained him as much respect and loyalty from his community as did his uncanny ability to get his followers out of dire situations alive.

By following Cheeseekau to the Chickamaugas and witnessing Dragging Canoe's alliance of resistance, Tecumseh had absorbed many lessons about fighting and building pan-tribal unity. He also grew up, as a man with a lover and child, and as a warrior with his first command. Now his role models, Cheeseekau and Dragging Canoe, were gone. By time he reached his home, Tecumseh was a war leader in his own right, known for fierce and inventive fighting against his enemies, generosity to his followers, and mercy to his captives. It must have seemed to him that, after years of struggling and suffering, his people in the Ohio country finally faced a most promising future after their recent military success. If so, he would soon learn that this was not the case.

Several factors combined to give the American Indians of the northwest a false sense of hope in 1792. Their remarkable victory in the recent battle against the United States was exhilarating. It was easy to believe, after a triumph against superior forces, that the native nations, working together, might be able to push the United States back, forcing its government to abandon its forts and its settlers to return to the east. Leaders imagined that they might reestablish the Proclamation of 1763 border of the Appalachians as the dividing line between the United States and Native America. Such rhetoric drew support from the British Indian agents who lived among the Shawnees and their neighbors. Officially, these men represented the British government. Personally, these agents' interests were inextricably tied up in the Native American community. Men such as Matthew Elliott and Alexander McKee traded with the American Indians, married into their families, and became fixtures in their towns, men of considerable influence and esteem. Both their official and personal ties led these agents to support any plans made against the United States.

The British Indian agents, who lived and worked among the Shawnees, might have been expected to sympathize closely with Native American sentiments against the United States. But the British contributed in another, more formal manner to the conflict between the Northwest Confederacy and the United States. As a matter of policy, the British had tarried, delaying departure from their posts on the U.S. side of the new border with the United States after the War of Independence. Although they did not help their former allies in a meaningful way during the period of the Conquest Treaties, they did provide supplies and gifts to the northern native nations in order to promote trade and peace along the Canadian line. In 1794, the British made an even bolder move by constructing Fort Miami on the lower Maumee River, near present-day Toledo. This new fortification, located so near the native nations, suggested a new, closer alliance with the Native American cause against the United States. In reality, the gesture had more to do with events in Europe than with those in North America. Great Britain, which was now at war with France, worried that the French might succeed in persuading American Indians to side with them against Britain. Fearing for their Canadian territories, British leaders prescribed goodwill with the Northwest Confederacy. Many Native leaders, however, interpreted this renewal of friendship as sanction and support for their side in the conflict to come with the United States.

In the wake of their military success and bolstered by encouragement, both real and imagined, from the British, the Shawnees successfully breathed new life into the confederacy Joseph Brant had first begun in 1783. They hosted a grand conference in October 1792 at the Glaize, where the Auglaize River connected to the Maumee River. The meeting was the single largest show of unity organized by Native Americans to date; representatives from more than two dozen native nations, from Canada, the Great Lakes region, the Ohio and Wabash Rivers, and the south, all gathered to discuss a unified resistance to U.S. expansionism. The Glaize became the de facto seat of the confederacy. Many key leaders lived in settlements nearby. Among the most important of the pan-tribal chiefs were the Shawnee leaders Kekewepelethy (Great Hawk), Blue Jacket, and Blacksnake, the Miami leader Little Turtle, the Delaware leader Buckongahelas, and the Ottawa leader Egushawa, who represented the Three Fires of the Ottawas, Ojibwes, and Potawatomis. British and French Indian agents and traders also made up a portion of the Glaize population.

Because of the military success they had won against U.S. soldiers, the idea of British support, and the tremendous renewal of pan-tribal cooperation, the representatives of the native nations were confident—or, more precisely, overconfident. They were not interested in surrendering to the demands of the United States, as represented by the treaties signed in 1789 at Fort Harmar, which ceded Native control of most of the Ohio country. Significantly, they proved equally uninterested in compromise, as represented by Joseph Brant's entreaties to negotiate a new boundary falling between the old 1763 border established by Britain and the 1789 border recognized by the United States. The confederacy leaders demanded nothing less than a full retreat of U.S. forces and settlers over the Appalachian Mountains. They believed themselves to be bargaining from a position of strength. Soon they would discover they were mistaken in this assumption.

Peace talks faltered, as it became clear that no compromise was possible. Even during the formal lull in hostilities, however, tensions ran high and bloodshed continued. For example, in April 1793, a group of unidentified American Indians crossed the Ohio River without formal orders or permission and attacked the fortification of Morgan's Station. The raid cost many U.S. lives. Because this was a solo effort by a few individuals, other Natives, including Tecumseh, were unaware that it was taking place. He was leading a hunting expedition not far away, a mixed group that included women and children. When rangers attempted to track down those responsible for the attack, they came across Tecumseh's hunting camp. They assumed that Tecumseh and his band were a war party traveling to Kentucky to make military strikes against the settlers there. The rangers surrounded Tecumseh's camp and launched a surprise attack after darkness fell. True to his reputation for fast thinking, Tecumseh managed to get the noncombatants out of harm's way and then directed his warriors to circle around their attackers and retreat with the rest of the party. His ability to assess dire situations coolly and devise strategies for saving his followers' lives won him tremendous renown among his people; such skills were needed in a time of instability and uncertainty.

Just because Tecumseh led a hunting party in this particular instance does not mean that he did not take part in border raids. He no doubt did his share of fighting as well as hunting during this period. Although Joseph Brant's vision for a pan-tribal confederacy had made a terrific impact on him, Tecumseh did not agree with Brant's call for moderation and compromise. He wished to push U.S. forces and settlers back toward the east. In 1794, he had even greater reason to hope that this might occur. In April of that year, the lieutenant governor of Upper Canada, John Graves Simcoe, made a speech to his Native American allies that included comments that were not approved by his superiors in London. Simcoe speculated that Great Britain would face war with the United States within the coming year. If Britain won, Simcoe suggested, its leaders would overturn the recent treaties so despised by the native nations and create an alliance with the confederacy. The news was welcome—but, unfortunately for Tecumseh and his people, completely unfounded.

The United States was not idle during this time. Two new forts appeared in Ohio: Fort Greenville, positioned near what is today Piqua, and Fort Recovery, located at the site of the army's recent defeat. News came to the Glaize that Major General Anthony Wayne had been stockpiling weapons and gathering soldiers, and now he planned to move his main force from Fort Greenville to Fort Recovery. To the Native leaders, this period of transit seemed to be an ideal time to strike. In June 1794, a force of American Indians from various confederacy nations and led by Blue Jacket went on the offensive to try to intercept these forces. Tecumseh and his band were among them. On June 30, the warriors attacked a U.S. convoy of hundreds of packhorses on its way to Fort Recovery. They captured some of the horses and drove the others away from their owners. The warriors killed approximately half of the soldiers who were escorting the animals and sent the rest fleeing to the fort, empty-handed.

Thus far, the raid was a strategic success. The warriors had interrupted the convoy, seized the pack animals, and either killed or turned back the troops. The overconfidence of some of the warriors, however, turned the victory into failure. While Tecumseh and his band, along with others, sought to secure the U.S. horses, others, such as the Ojibwes and the Ottawas, decided to press their advantage. Buoyed by the day's success, they chose to continue on to Fort Recovery and launch an ambitious attack. The idea was ill conceived: the warriors were more than a match for moving convoy, but they could not breach a secure fortress. They wasted ammunition and energy in the failed strike. The defeat halted the momentum that the confederacy had enjoyed; worse still, it introduced new discord among the native nations. Those warriors who attacked Fort Recovery accused the others, including the Delawares and the Shawnees who had focused on securing the captured horses, of cowardice. The strike had failed, the attackers claimed, because the other warriors had not provided proper assistance. In reply, the Delawares and the Shawnees protested that the attack had been rash, foolish, poorly planned, and contrary to the tactics upon which they had agreed. The alliance disintegrated, and approximately one-third of the confederacy forces abandoned the pan-tribal army.

While internal disputes tore apart the native nations, Major General Wayne saw an opportunity to exploit his enemies' vulnerability. In August, roughly 3,500 U.S. soldiers marched on the heart of the confederacy, the Glaize. The Shawnees and their neighbors were forced to retreat, deserting their homes and their fields of maturing crops. They fell back to Swan Creek, near present-day Toledo, which had the benefit of being close to the British at Fort Miami. With the reassurance of British allies near, a force of Shawnees, Wyandots, Potawatomis, Ottawas, Ojibwes, and private British and Canadian volunteers gathered. They made a stand against the United States at a decimated spot that had been savaged by a tornado and was thereafter called Fallen Timbers. The armies met on August 20. The Native Americans were outnumbered nearly three to one.

Tecumseh and his warriors acquitted themselves well. They hid in the grass, emerging when a line of Kentuckians drew near, attacking the soldiers and sending them back in broken ranks, confused and disoriented. When Tecumseh's rifle jammed, he continued fighting with a fowler, unwilling to yield. As the main body of the confederacy forces retreated, he and his men repeatedly fell back to form new lines and hold them as long as possible, until they were finally forced to withdraw or be outflanked by the U.S. soldiers. The defeat was bitter.

The Battle of Fallen Timbers proved to be disastrous for the Native Americans for a number of reasons. The clear and decisive U.S. victory deflated the hope and confidence that had animated the latest incarnation of the confederacy. The very fact that the American Indians had made their defense with depleted numbers, because those disaffected by the Fort Recovery strike had abandoned their neighbors and withdrawn from the alliance, offered proof that unity was already lost—and that, once divided, the native nations could be conquered. But the aftermath of the battle itself provided the harshest blow to Tecumseh and his comrades. As the warriors retreated from Fallen Timbers, they made their way to the only haven of safety they had left: Fort Miami. The British had courted the native nations as allies and had suggested that war between Britain and the United States was imminent. Even the location of the British fort spoke volumes to the Shawnees, the Delawares, and others about the close ties they shared with their British supporters. But when the defeated warriors fell back to Fort Miami, however, they found its doors locked to them. The commanding officer, Major William Campbell, did not dare risk a U.S. attack on his fortification, and so he left his would-be allies standing at his gates, without shelter or support. The warriors were furious at what they felt to be British betrayal and treachery. And so the Battle of Fallen Timbers ended in resentment and humiliation for the Native Americans. The Northwest Confederacy had fought the United States for control of the Northwest Territory for a decade, but this final defeat ended the conflict alternately known as Little Turtle's War or the Northwest Indian War.

Beyond marking the end of a long-standing struggle, the Battle of Fallen Timbers held special significance for Tecumseh, although he did not realize it at the time. Just as he fought for the Shawnees and their allies in the conflict, another young man of roughly his same age fought for his country on the opposing side. The Battle of Fallen Timbers was the first time Tecumseh and William Henry Harrison fought on the same battlefield. Harrison was a Virginian of impressive and powerful family. His father was a delegate to the Continental Congress, a signer of the

Declaration of Independence, and governor of Virginia. His father-in-law was a U.S. congressman. At the time of the Battle of Fallen Timbers, Harrison served as aide-de-camp to General Wayne. Soon he would leave the U.S. Army and launch his political career in the Northwest Territory. He would build his personal and professional reputation, which eventually won him the U.S. presidency, on his status as Tecumseh's opponent.

In 1794, however, Tecumseh had no understanding of how Harrison would become a major figure in his own life and movement. The cause Tecumseh had supported, the Northwest Confederacy, seemed lost. It was no doubt difficult to think beyond this defeat. Frustrated and embittered, Tecumseh chose to hunt with a small traveling party through the winter of 1794–1795, withdrawing from Shawnee and pan-tribal politics and focusing on the basics of food and shelter. His impressive leadership skills continued to contribute to his reputation, despite his modest goals. His generosity toward those under his protection was widely known, as was his special attention to the needs of the aged, infirm, and vulnerable. Circulating stories about him underscored his abilities as a provider and protector. Now, as he hunted, he did nothing to hide his dissatisfaction with the current condition of his people; he refused to meet with British agents or rebuild the homes lost in the most recent wave of attacks.

Tecumseh did not attend the meeting on August 3, 1795, that produced the Treaty of Greenville. Representatives of all the native nations related to the lands in question were present, including the Shawnees, as were U.S. officials. William Henry Harrison was one of the U.S. signers of the agreement. The treaty offered indisputable evidence that the Northwest Confederacy possessed no bargaining power; the agreement not only affirmed the past land cessions but also extended U.S. authority over new areas in present-day Ohio state. Among those who signed were war chiefs familiar to Tecumseh: Little Turtle, Egushawa, Buckongahelas, Blue Jacket, and Red Pole, as well as the Shawnee civil chief Black Hoof, or Catecahassa. Black Hoof was significantly older than Tecumseh—he claimed to have been at the Battle of Monongahela during the French and Indian War, in 1755—but he does not enter the historical record clearly until the signing of the Treaty of Greenville. Like William Henry Harrison, Black Hoof would become a foil for Tecumseh and an obstacle to his plans. Unlike Tecumseh, Black Hoof advocated cultural adaptation and alliance with the United States as the most practical means by which the Shawnees could survive.

Tecumseh did not agree with Black Hoof's perspective or with the choice he and his fellow chiefs made to sign the treaty. Blue Jacket visited Tecumseh's camp personally to explain the treaty and the reasons he had agreed to it; the fact that such a prominent leader felt it necessary to explain himself and to try to win Tecumseh's approval signaled Tecumseh's growing status as a leader. Despite Blue Jacket's entreaties, however, Tecumseh would not visit a U.S. fort or make any other show of support for the agreement.

Some who were not already followers of Tecumseh became so because of his consistent stand against land cession. Tecumseh's band grew to 45 or 50 warriors; with their families, they made a large enough group to warrant their own community. And so, in 1796, Tecumseh and his followers set up a new village on the Great Miami River near Piqua today. Among the members were Tecumseh's brothers Kumskaukau and Lalawéthika and probably his sister, Tecumapease, and her husband, Wahsikegaboe. After a year's planting and harvesting, Tecumseh relocated the community west to the Whitewater River, in present-day Indiana. Tecumseh's withdrawal from his former neighbors was intellectual as well as physical. The former seat of the Northwest Confederacy had degenerated into a field of factions. The peace party included Blue Jacket, Red Pole, and others, while Kekewepelethy led the party against the United States. After Britain complied with Jay's Treaty and abandoned Detroit and Fort Miami, the center of Shawnee politics moved to Wapakoneta, on the Auglaize River near Fort Defiant.

Although Tecumseh was a Shawnee leader of Shawnee followers, his vision transcended his narrow affiliation. He remained outside, or above, Shawnee politics and governance. His detractors later pointed out that he never sat on the Shawnee tribal council, and this was true. He dreamed of one day reuniting the scattered factions of the Shawnees, but he lived and fought beside American Indians from many different native nations. And, in 1798, he relocated his people once more, this time to another setting with diverse neighbors. He gained permission from the local Delawares to move northwest—each move took him ever farther away from U.S. expansion—to the west fork of the White River, northwest of present-day Hamilton, Indiana. The site boasted plentiful game and excellent farming land. The nearby communities included a Nanticoke village and nine Delaware villages. This fertile and friendly place served as Tecumseh's home for nearly a decade.

Even though Tecumseh set himself apart from the center of Shawnee political life, older leaders recognized his unique gifts and began to call upon him in times of tension. One such instance came during a frontier crisis in 1799. Peace always was fragile on the borders between U.S. and Native communities and often between the native nations themselves. In

1799, a rumor reached the Shawnees that the Chickasaws, to the south-east, were planning an attack against them. The Chickasaws' alleged motive was revenge for the death of Chickasaws who had acted as U.S. scouts during fighting between the United States and the Shawnees five years earlier. There was no truth to these rumors of Chickasaw reprisal against the Shawnees, but the Shawnees took the threat seriously at the time. They mobilized their warriors and arranged for safe havens for their dependents. U.S. settlers, however, viewed this Shawnee activity with alarm, imagining that the Shawnees were preparing for an offensive strike against them. Two white settlers, William Ward and Simon Kenton, sent a query to the village of Wapakoneta asking about Shawnee intentions. After various messages passed back and forth, both sides agreed on a meeting. The Shawnee leaders chose Tecumseh as the primary spokesman for his people. He reassured the settlers of the Shawnees' peaceful intentions toward them. According to Benjamin Drake's 1841 biography, Tecumseh "made a speech on that occasion, which was much admired for its force and eloquence. The interpreter, Dechouset, said that he found it very difficult to translate the lofty flights of Tecumseh."[1]

Tecumseh's reputation as a statesman and orator was put to the test yet again in April 1803. Friction grew between the Anglo and the Native communities because of two deaths. A white settler was murdered not far from his home near Chillicothe; because he was scalped, his neighbors suspected that his murderer was Native American. In retaliation, some of them captured and killed an American Indian man, although they had no proof—or even suspicion—that he was the one personally responsible for the settler's death. Other settlers, like their Native counterparts, feared that the cycle of vengeful killing would escalate into a state of war. Knowing of his renown and authority, a group of whites sought out Tecumseh. He denounced the original killing of the U.S. settler and denied that any of his people were responsible. At the community's request, he formally addressed the Anglo community via an interpreter and shared his message of peace. His actions restored calm to both sides, averting what might have been a bloody conflict. Benjamin Drake based his 1841 description of Tecumseh's address from firsthand accounts: "'When Tecumseh rose to speak,' says an eyewitness, 'as he cast his gaze over the vast multitude, which the interesting occasion had drawn together, he appeared one of the most dignified men I ever beheld. While this orator of nature was speaking, the vast crowds preserved the most profound silence. From the confident manner in which he spoke of the intention of the Indians to adhere to the treaty of Greenville, and live in peace and friendship with their white brethren, he dispelled, as if by magic, the apprehensions of the whites.'"[2]

Concentrating on the community he had founded and its peoples' welfare, not to mention larger issues of the Shawnees and Native Americans a whole, left little time for Tecumseh to focus on his personal life. During this relatively settled decade, however, Tecumseh did make two attempts at wedlock. First, he married Mamate, a woman of mixed Shawnee-Anglo descent. By all accounts, she was considered unusually beautiful and desirable; despite this, Tecumseh apparently married her more out of a sense of obligation than affection. The position of chief was not necessarily hereditary, and so Tecumseh did not technically need an heir. Yet, any ideal Shawnee man was the father of at least one son who would grow up to take his father's (or grandfather's) place as a warrior. Tecumseh already was a father, but his daughter lived among the Cherokees. Perhaps the desire or pressure for another child, one raised within his family and preferably a boy, led Tecumseh to marry. Mamate and Tecumseh had a son, Paukeesaa ("A Cat Stalking Its Prey"), in 1796. Tecumseh terminated the marriage shortly thereafter. According to interviews with friends and comrades, Mamate could not live up to Tecumseh's exacting expectations. No record remains of Manate's fate, but by the age of seven or eight, Paukeesaa lived not by his mother but with Tecumseh's sister, Tecumapease, who became his primary caregiver. Tecumseh and Paukeesaa never shared a comfortable relationship, although their paths grew closer in the last months of Tecumseh's life.

Tecumseh's next marriage was to White Wing, or Wa-be-le-gu-ne-qua, roughly five years after his divorce of Mamate. It was a prestigious match; White Wing was the daughter of the Shawnee chief Half Moon, and her position brought additional weight to Tecumseh's status as a leader. The union appeared to be amicable, yet it survived only until 1807. Perhaps the childlessness of the marriage contributed to its ultimate failure. There would be no more marriages or children for Tecumseh. The relatively quiet interlude he enjoyed as chief of his settlement drew to a close, as changing events demanded Tecumseh's attention.

While Tecumseh tried to build a new life for himself and his followers on the White River, William Henry Harrison, now the governor of Indiana Territory, stayed busy. His primary mandate was to encourage more U.S. citizens to move west and occupy the land in preparation for statehood. This meant that more Native Americans had to be moved from their territories. Harrison was not overly discriminating about the manner in which he accomplished this. Between 1802 and 1805, he arranged for seven land cession treaties that secured present-day Illinois, portions of Missouri and Wisconsin, and southern Indiana for the United States. In return for these lands, the native nations received a maximum of two cents an acre, and sometimes less. U.S. officials used questionable and at times clearly illegal methods to convince the Native leaders to acquiesce. For example, some chiefs were bought with bribes or confused with alcohol; others were warned that the annuities promised to their people as part of past treaty agreements would not be paid unless the new treaty was signed. In other cases, the U.S. officials made treaties with individuals who were neither the owners nor the representatives of the owners of the land in question.

The new treaties exacerbated the divisions among and within the native nations. Distrust and anger grew between those who were consulted about a given land cession and those who were not, those who blamed leaders who agreed to the treaties and those who did not, those who pledged to ignore the treaties as illegitimate and those who did not, and those who were committed to pushing back the white settlers and those who were not. Some chiefs were so shamed by their complicity in the treaties that they tried to keep the details of the agreements secret from their people. The Shawnees made few concessions during this period, but Tecumseh watched others, including his neighbors the Delawares, surrender lands and grow increasingly insecure in their lives and property. Initial payments for land sales offered a temporary solution for poverty at the price of internal strife. When the money was gone and the people had even less land from which to make their living, selling more land provided another short-term answer, while igniting further factionalism, and the pattern continued. And the situation was growing ever more complicated. In 1803, the United States purchased the Louisiana Territory, which meant that the native nations were now effectively surrounded. Moving west no longer meant moving out of the reach of U.S. forces or white settlers.

Added to Native American unrest and uncertainty was a new source of instability and danger: disease. An outbreak in 1802 affected all of the communities up and down the White River and hit the Delawares particularly hard. In 1804–1805, another outbreak followed a devastatingly cold winter and torrential floods. Many illnesses plagued the communities; perhaps the most deadly was smallpox. Disease claimed the life of the revered Delaware chief Buckongahelas in 1805. His death seemed to mark the end of an era, the end of the promise of pan-tribal unity and Native power. It seemed that all that remained was shame and suffering. Tecumseh had earned the position of a trusted and respected leader, but he could do little to protect his people from plague.

The Shawnees, the Delawares, the Wyandots, and their neighbors all wondered whom to blame and what to do as the crises seemed to multiply. They received an answer from an unlikely source. No one could have been more surprised than Tecumseh.

NOTES

1. Quoted in C. F. Klinck, ed., *Tecumseh: Fact and Fiction in Early Records* (Ottawa: Tecumseh Press, 1978), p. 29.

2. Ibid., pp. 29–30.

Chapter 4

THE RISE OF THE PROPHET

No one expected much from Tecumseh's younger brother, Lalawéthika. Although he had grown up with Tecumseh and shared his travels, little of Tecumseh's sterling reputation had rubbed off on the young man whom many still remembered by his childhood nickname of "Noisy Rattle." The two brothers hardly could have been more different. Tecumseh was an impressive figure; his close friends and allies, casual acquaintances, and even enemies remarked that he was unusually handsome, with a finely carved face and figure and a noble bearing. Despite the limp from his earlier injury—which few of those who recorded their impressions even noticed, or at least recalled—the adult Tecumseh commanded attention and respect when he entered a scene before he uttered a word. He complemented his handsome appearance with plain, simple attire. He wore his dark hair either long with a turban or shaved to the skull with one long scalp lock. His customary clothes included fringed buckskin pieces or a plain shirt with belted leggings and moccasins. Like other Shawnee men, his ears and nose were pierced; unlike many Shawnee men, however, he had no tattoos, although he applied red and black face paint on special occasions. By this time he was known as a compelling orator as well as a chief. Exceptionally well spoken, Tecumseh chose his words carefully, with great seriousness of purpose. His actions as a warrior and leader proved he was brave and coolly intelligent, as well as generous with his followers, merciful to his enemies, and consistently responsible for those he considered to be under his care.

Conversely, Lalawéthika was unimpressive in almost every possible way. He was of average height and slight build. He wore constant proof of his lack of physical prowess; as a clumsy child, he accidentally put out his own eye with an arrow, leaving his face permanently disfigured. According to some reports, his older brother Cheeseekau refused to train the inept youth because he believed Lalawéthika lacked the qualities necessary to be a Shawnee warrior. Apparently he did little enough fighting. Even when he was of age, he remained at times with the women and children rather than join his fellow young men in warfare; some reports suggest he did attend the Battle of Fallen Timbers but ultimately ran from the field. Accounts suggest that he overcompensated for his shortcomings by speaking loudly and often, allegedly bragging and lying. By adulthood, his reputation seems to have reached beyond his immediate Shawnee village; members of neighboring communities considered him to be scheming, ill tempered, deceitful, drunken, and slovenly. Unlike his older brother, Lalawéthika practiced polygamy. He worked when possible with herbs and remedies as a minor healer, but he depended on friends and family to help support his wives and children. Of course, it could not have been easy to grow up in the shadow first of Cheeseekau and then of Tecumseh, but Lalawéthika's twin, Kumskaukau, seems to have been regarded as an able warrior and worthy man. Lalawéthika, on the other hand, was an infamous outcast.

If Tecumseh the chief embodied the promise of a united Native American future, Lalawéthika the misfit reflected some of the social ills of his people at the time. The Shawnees faced a corporate identity crisis; not only did Anglo and Native American practices collide within the Shawnee nation but also the loss of land, number of relocations, and continued period of warfare undermined, or at least altered, traditional Shawnee ways. Many intermediary institutions that had evolved in Shawnee society suddenly dissolved or changed radically. For example, in the past the Shawnee nation had subdivided into five distinct groups, each with separate assigned roles within the Shawnee community as a whole. Now these internal designations meant very little. Tecumseh's career illustrates this clearly. External relations of the Shawnee nation, and therefore leadership of the Shawnee nation as a whole, traditionally fell to the Mekoches. Tecumseh and his siblings were, like their father, Kispokos. Tecumseh nonetheless had been chosen to represent the Shawnees to non-Shawnees on many occasions, and he later would make a bid for an even greater leadership role. His designation as a Kispoko posed no obstacle. It did not hinder his role, his support, or his aspirations. For Tecumseh, this was a good thing, of course, but such change and mobility also brought uncertainty about the proper roles of different groups within Shawnee society.

Furthermore, clear demarcations had once existed between Shawnee war leaders and civil leaders, and now those two authorities combined in the form of chiefs who exerted authority both at home and at war—for, indeed, the Shawnees had been in an almost constant state of war for many years. This destabilized the power structure of Shawnee villages and communities and made individual leaders far more powerful than they had been previously.

Perhaps most important, the classic Shawnee division of labor was undermined. In the past, Shawnee women had farmed and produced household goods, while Shawnee men had hunted and fought as warriors. However, as the colonies, and later the United States, expanded west the Shawnees had left cultivated fields time and again when villages were attacked or communities relocated for their safety. The women abandoned their harvests and had to cultivate new fields. Growing dependence on trade goods such as fabrics, tools, and weapons from white traders—British, French, or U.S.—also shifted control of supplies from female home manufacturers to male traders. As the Shawnees lost their lands, they also lost access to some hunting grounds and the assurance of safety in others. Moreover, the United States put significant pressure on the Shawnees and other native nations to alter their long-standing practices and adopt European ways. This "civilization campaign" was best represented by Secretary of State-turned-President Thomas Jefferson, who argued that the Native Americans could not hope to coexist with U.S. citizens unless they acculturated. One of the primary signs of "civilization," he claimed, was an agricultural economy run not by women but by men. The result of changes, or the threat of changes, in the traditional Shawnee division of labor was confusion and resentment.

The most significant factor of all in the Shawnee identity crisis, and in Lalawéthika's questionable character, was alcohol. Despite the fact the United States passed a law in 1802 forbidding the sale of liquor to American Indians, traders offered alcohol in constant and steady supply. Liquor was not a traditional element of Shawnee culture, and, paired with despair, anger, and hopelessness, it caused significant suffering. Shawnees and non-Shawnees alike complained of rampant alcoholism and related violence and domestic abuse. Young men who had grown up with dreams of being ideal Shawnee men, successful warriors and hunters and who now had the opportunity to do neither as they had been taught were particularly likely to become excessive drinkers. Lalawéthika, who did not fit into his community, could barely provide for his family, and failed to meet traditional Shawnee ideals was an extreme case, to be sure, but not an unusual example of the Shawnee dilemma writ large. Furthermore, he offered a clear case study of why the situation had to change for the Shawnees if they were to survive.

The Shawnee chief Black Hoof embodied one response to this cultural crisis. He believed that Shawnee culture had to change in order to escape complete destruction. On three separate occasions between 1803 and 1809, he led a delegation of Shawnees to Washington, D.C., to meet with the secretary of war, the cabinet official who at the time was responsible for U.S.-Native American relations. Black Hoof repeatedly requested assistance for his people in acculturating to the Anglo lifestyle. The Shawnees needed supplies and training in order to adopt the practices of U.S. citizens, he explained. His requests met mixed success, but he employed what help he received with diligence. He and his followers began to build permanent log cabins for year-round habitation. These replaced the light, open summer homes and the domed, bark winter homes the Shawnees typically used. They began to implement male farming with machinery to replace female farming with digging sticks. They began also to introduce domesticated livestock for food to replace the hunt for wild game.

Although Black Hoof was willing to sacrifice Shawnee traditions to accommodate U.S. demands, he was just as adamant in his own way as Tecumseh was about protecting Shawnee lands. In fact, he believed his approach was far likelier to persuade the United States to protect Shawnee property rights. He petitioned the U.S. government for a deed or legal document of some kind to prove that the Shawnees could remain in western Ohio if they invested such tremendous time and effort in adopting white ways. U.S. officials such as Henry Dearborn refused to commit themselves, however, realizing that further U.S. expansion was imminent. Black Hoof continued to ask for assurances about his people's land, and in the meantime he helped his people in Wapakoneta with the cultural transition effort. Among those who trained Black Hoof's Shawnees in agricultural practices was the Quaker missionary William Kirk, who also established a mission in the Shawnee village.

Black Hoof's accommodationist approach was not the only response to the Shawnee crisis, however, nor was the crisis confined to the Shawnees. Instability in the culture and insecurity in land ownership combined with waves of dreaded diseases to create a volatile situation for the Shawnees and their neighbors. Among the Shawnee allies the Delawares, illness took many lives. An elderly woman named Beata who lived in one of the Delaware towns on the White River, not far from Tecumseh, proclaimed that she could explain what was happening. Her revelation reflected a blend of Native American and Christian religions. As a child, Beata had been baptized in a Moravian village, but she had not been a member of a Christian church or even associated with missionaries in many years. She professed faith in the Great Spirit (Waashaa Monetoo), who was recognized by both the Delawares and the Shawnees as the benevolent creator of all.

The disease and death plaguing the region, Beata claimed, represented the Great Spirit's judgment on the American Indians for abandoning their traditional lifestyles and becoming debauched and degenerate. The people themselves had opened their communities to evil practices and earned this terrible retribution, she explained. Her story seemed to incorporate elements of Christian theology, because she claimed that the Great Spirit would soon send a messiah figure to model the right way to live and deliver the people from damnation into righteousness. Her identification of the culprits who had enraged the Great Spirit, however, came from a distinctly Native American perspective. She blamed first the bad behavior of the Delawares and their neighbors, especially when fueled by alcohol. Other culprits were whites—all whites, not only U.S. soldiers and settlers but also missionaries and traders. Beata additionally named the chiefs who had ceded land as the particular focus of the Great Spirit's anger.

The second part of Beata's message also appeared to incorporate traditional beliefs along with distinctly Christian influences. She claimed that she had experienced a revelation from the Great Spirit. An apocalypse was coming to destroy the wicked, she said. In the meantime, however, witches had infiltrated the villages, poisoning the people and making an already bad situation even worse. Delawares, Shawnees, and other neighboring native nations believed in sorcery and the dark magic that witches, both men and women, could perform. The idea of apocalypse, however, had more in common with Christianity. Beata promised that she could identify witches in the community. If the people wanted to gain favor with the Great Spirit and avoid a terrible fate when the apocalypse arrived, they would have to purge these witches from their midst. In short, Beata called for a witch-hunt and the execution of the guilty.

Tecumseh's brother Lalawéthika had reasons to be deeply affected by Beata's revelations. First, they were a direct response to the dire illnesses that plagued the Delawares. Lalawéthika was a healer, although not an especially successful or respected one; still, he knew the disease better than most and recognized that it was taking hold of Tecumseh's village, threatening Shawnee lives. If Beata's words applied to those who were dispossessed of their land only to be struck by disease, they were as relevant to the Shawnees as the Delawares. More to the point, Lalawéthika was a living example of many of the things Beata criticized about Native Americans. He could not be called the model of traditional Shawnee masculinity; he did not hold to traditional ways. Worse still, he was an alcoholic and a family disgrace. Perhaps he feared that Beata was correct and his behavior had infuriated the Great Spirit and brought calamity to his people. Perhaps he worried that others would draw the same conclusion. Whatever his feelings, Lalawéthika could not remain indifferent.

Some time in 1805—accounts differ as to the date and details—Lalawéthika had a vision of his own. Whether this was a dream he experienced while sleeping or a revelation he experienced while awake is uncertain. The details he related of his vision, however, are well documented. Possibly feeling guilty about his life and/or frightened for the future, Lalawéthika foresaw his own death. His soul traveled down a path and came to a fork. One route seemed to go to a glorious afterlife of peace and joy, and he saw some American Indians ahead of him on that path headed for heavenly contentment. The other route led to a terrible place of damnation, and he saw other Native Americans following that path to eternal torment and suffering. He even identified some of these tortured souls as witches, drunkards, and wife beaters. Rather than continue his journey into the afterlife, Lalawéthika retraced his steps and returned to the living in order to warn his people about what he had seen and to exhort them to proper behavior. As he began to tell others of his vision, he claimed that the Great Spirit had chosen him as a conduit of holy revelations for the betterment of the Shawnees and all American Indians. In effect, he admitted to being Beata's promised messianic figure. To mark his new role, he renamed himself Tenskwatawa, "The Open Door." Believers, however, soon called him simply the Prophet.

According to those who knew him, Lalawéthika underwent a radical transformation as he became the Prophet. He trembled with emotion as he addressed his people and shed tears when he recounted his vision. Tecumseh was hardly the only one astounded by the remarkable change in his brother. To his detractors, the Prophet's unimpressive past as Lalawéthika made his new incarnation as a holy man highly suspicious. To his followers, however, the dramatic contrast between his lifestyle before his vision and after it proved the power and authenticity of his revelation.

His prescription for right living was somewhat paradoxical, as it urged a return to traditional ways while introducing new ones. Just as Beata had done, the Prophet blended elements of Native American and Christian religions, whether he intended to or not, in order to create a new spiritual teaching. For example, the Prophet incorporated the ideas of a heaven and hell in the afterlife—places of eternal reward and punishment, respectively—into his theology, despite the fact the religion of the Shawnees and their neighbors had not previously possessed these concepts. He urged his people to live the proper life so that they could spend eternity in contentment rather than torture. The proper life included embracing what it meant to be American Indian and living separately in every way from the whites.

Practically speaking, this meant that American Indians should revive ancient ceremonies and seek to be self-sufficient, rather than depend on traders and European-style goods. They should live as their ancestors had, eating indigenous meals (rather than pork, chicken, wheat, and other foods that colonists had brought with them) and following traditional lifestyles (farming and pursuing home manufacturing as they had in the past and not according to the designs of any imposed civilization campaign). Moreover, American Indians had to abandon new and undesirable practices such as drinking alcohol and practicing polygamy. The Prophet claimed that the Great Spirit had made the forests of North America for American Indians only and that they had every right to stay on the land, protect it, and make their living from it. To do otherwise was to deny the will of the Creator.

Even as the Prophet urged his people to look to tradition for the model of the good life, he instructed individuals to make a break with their sinful pasts. He recommended that each person follow two steps in order to do this. First, he said, individuals should destroy their personal medicine bags. This was highly controversial, because a medicine bag was considered to be something very important, sacred, and private. It held items that reminded its owner of the guardian spirit that offered guidance and protection throughout his or her life. The Prophet was asking for a significant sacrifice indeed. Furthermore, the Prophet proclaimed that American Indians needed to confess their wrongdoings. Since he was the chosen vessel of the Great Spirit's will, the Prophet stated that he and a group of his choosing would hear the confessions personally. Again, this reflected a significant break with past customs. It also concentrated a great deal of power in the hands of the Prophet. If some chose not to give up their medicine bags or confess their evil acts, they might be suspected of being witches—and, as Beata's witch-hunt already proved, the punishment for witchcraft was death.

To some, the Prophet's teaching seemed solely like self-aggrandizement. As the only interpreter of God's will, the Prophet could devise wholly new ceremonies and exercise what amounted to the power of life and death over his people. He had risen almost overnight from being a community misfit and family embarrassment to become a broker of souls. Yet to many others, the Prophet's words brought hope. His revelation included a vision of the future in which supernatural powers would overthrow the whites in North America as well as the sinful Native Americans, leaving the land and replenished game for the faithful American Indians to enjoy in peace and prosperity. For many of those who were dispossessed of their land, disheartened about their changing culture, and disturbed by the spread of disease, the Prophet offered clear calls to action and promises for a better tomorrow. Significantly, despite his rhetoric against Anglo culture, the Prophet advocated peace, not war; he believed that superhuman forces, and not earthly warriors, would defeat the whites forever.

The Prophet's teachings followed immediately in the pattern of the Delaware woman Beata's and complemented them. His beliefs also fit in a larger tradition of American Indian prophecy and nativism. Since first contact with Europeans, in fact, different Native religious figures had blamed death and disorder on the people's disobedience and had foretold fantastic ways in which the Europeans would disappear from the continent and traditional life would return. Closer to the Prophet's time, two spiritual leaders in particular had reflected this tradition: the Munsee prophet Wangomend, whose movement lasted roughly from 1752 to 1775, and the Delaware prophet Neolin, whose movement lasted roughly from 1760 to 1766. If the Prophet's movement diverged from the older tradition of religious nativism, it did so by coming at an unparalleled time of crisis for the Shawnees and their neighbors, thanks to social instability, political defeat, and widespread disease, and by blending Christian doctrine with traditional native religion.

Despite the fact that the Prophet worked within an established tradition of Native American prophecy and nativism, he quickly faced opposition from important American Indian leaders. Many of the Shawnee leaders from Wapakoneta and its surrounding area resented what they perceived as the Prophet's attempt to usurp their rightful authority. Knowing Lalawéthika's past reputation, they also mistrusted his sudden change of heart and message of salvation. Black Hoof, Blackbeard, Black Snake, Piaseka the Wolf (the son of the revered Cornstalk), and others found the Prophet to be suspect, even dangerous. To be sure, the Prophet's actions played into the fears of his enemies. The Delawares who lived on the White River sent for the Prophet to give assistance to Beata as she tried to cleanse their people of their wickedness. He answered the summons and became a witch-hunter among the Delawares, accusing various individuals of sorcery and dark magic. At his word, some were tortured for their confessions, and others were executed. After a time, his efforts inspired a backlash. Some claimed that young would-be leaders among the Delawares were exploiting the investigation of witches as a means of undermining the older, entrenched leadership elite. The Prophet eventually left the Delawares in a state of political chaos. When the Wyandots and Senecas on the Sandusky River requested the Prophet's assistance in similar purgings, he acquiesced, only to be rejected when he accused some of the communities' most respected members of sorcery. For a time he continued identifying witches from afar. He even dared to suggest that the Shawnee leadership in Wapakoneta had sorcerers among its ranks.

The Wapakoneta Shawnees were not the only ones who feared that the Prophet might represent a destabilizing influence in nearby Native American communities. U.S. officials were concerned about his teachings and especially his role in the deadly witch-hunts. To them, he represented an obstacle to the U.S. policy of "civilizing" the native nations. Governor William Henry Harrison of Indiana was particularly concerned about what the Prophet's movement might mean. On April 18, 1805, he sent a message to the American Indians in his region, claiming that the Prophet was both a charlatan and a danger to them:

> My children: My heart is filled with grief and my eyes are dissolved in tears at the news which has reached me. You have been celebrated for your wisdom above all the tribes of the red people who inhabit this great island. Your fame as warriors has extended to the remotest nations, and the wisdom of your chiefs has gained you the appellation of grandfathers from all the neighboring tribes. From what cause, then, does it proceed that you have departed from the wise council of your fathers, and covered yourselves with guilt? My children, tread back the steps you have taken, and endeavor to regain the straight road you have abandoned. The dark, crooked and thorny one which you are now pursuing will certainly lead to endless woe and misery. But who is this pretended prophet who dares to in the name of the great Creator? Examine him. Is he more wise and virtuous than you are yourselves, that he should be selected to convey to you the orders of your God? Demand of him some proof at least of his being the messenger of the Deity. If God has really employed him, He has doubtless authorized him to perform miracles that he may be known and received as a prophet. If he is really a prophet, ask him to cause the sun to stand still, or the moon to alter its courses, the river to cease to flow or the dead to rise from their graves. If he does these things you may believe that he is sent from God. He tells you that the Great

Spirit commands you to punish with death those who deal in
magic, and that he is authorized to point them out. Wretched
delusion! Is, then, the Master of Life compelled to employ
mortal man to punish those who offend Him? Has He not the
thunder and the power of nature at his command? And could
not He sweep away from the earth the whole nation at one motion of His arm? My children, do not believe that the great and
good Creator has directed you to destroy your own flesh, and
do not doubt that if you pursue this abominable wickedness,
His vengeance will overtake you and crush you.[1]

He hoped his words would undermine the credibility of the Prophet. Harrison's challenge was not exactly useful to his cause, however. A total eclipse
of the sun occurred on June 16. The Prophet assembled the faithful and
took credit for the event. The Prophet's reputation spread despite—and
because of—Harrison's challenge.

The Prophet's repeated emphasis on reclaiming American Indian identity and dignity appealed to some who were not altogether taken with his
theology. Tecumseh certainly appreciated the usefulness of the Prophet's
ideas. After Lalawéthika became Tenskwatawa, Tecumseh made modest
changes that reflected his support for his brother's invocation of the past.
For example, he changed his diet so that he ate mostly indigenous foods,
and he abstained from alcohol completely. Tecumseh's transformation
was marked by moderation and practicality, however; he dressed more
conservatively, but he did not altogether abandon wearing European or
U.S.-style manufactured cloth, and he continued using weapons such as
muskets that had to be obtained by trade with whites. It seems clear that
he was not a true believer in all aspects of the Prophet's religious movement. He did, however, appreciate that the Prophet's message of social
and cultural revitalization and his call to separateness and self-sufficiency
were additional tools that could be used in achieving his own dreams of
Shawnee reunification and pan-tribal unity.

Together, Tecumseh and the Prophet agreed to found a new community. Ostensibly, the reason for this was to build a base for the Prophet's religious movement. Tecumseh, however, saw a bigger picture: he imagined
that establishing the village and promoting the faith would lay the foundation for his plan for political unification. The brothers chose Greenville,
Ohio, which not only was the site of a treaty they both regretted but also
was situated on the U.S. side of the border. They believed that their location would help to communicate their peaceful intentions; after all, they
were not hidden or secretive, but rather nearby and visible, and Shawnees

would not move their families to a site where they expected hostilities to erupt. Repeatedly they explained that they sought no war with the United States, only internal reform within their own peoples. They invited their neighbors and followers to join them.

Tecumseh's first goal was to bring together the fragmented Shawnee nation. By this time, five major Shawnee communities survived. One was Tecumseh's village in Indiana territory. Another was located north in Michigan, and the remaining three were situated in various places in Ohio. Tecumseh dreamed of convincing other groups to relocate to Greenville, so the Shawnees would be one people once again. Of course, this call from Tecumseh, this invitation welcoming other communities into his own, implied that Tecumseh would continue to serve as the leader of the new settlement, in effect the principal chief of the reassembled Shawnee nation. His ambition and daring were great, and this made him powerful enemies. Black Hoof remained the primary voice of opposition. Together, Tecumseh and Black Hoof represented very different visions of the future for the Shawnees, visions that could not be reconciled. Without Black Hoof's support, Tecumseh could not be the architect of Shawnee reunification. And Black Hoof's support did not appear to be forthcoming.

Support did arrive from other, unexpected directions, however. Blue Jacket, the legendary Shawnee war leader and diplomat, gave his approval to the brothers' new venture. Because of his visibility and reputation, this meant a great deal. Soon non-Shawnees responded to the promise of Greenville. Chief Roundhead and his Wyandots from the upper Scioto River, for example, took up permanent residence in the village. Visitors came from near and far, and, as they returned to their homes, they spread the word about what was happening in the settlement and the movement it represented. Kickapoos who had grown tired of the growing numbers of white settlers in Illinois journeyed to Greenville in such large numbers that William Henry Harrison sent word to the Kickapoo chiefs, telling them to keep their people at home. Embarrassed and chagrined, the chiefs admitted that they had tried and been unsuccessful. They could not compete, it seemed, with the attraction of the Prophet's message and Tecumseh's community.

U.S. policy assisted the Greenville enterprise. Officials continued to negotiate additional treaties with native nations in order to secure more land for westward expansion. When chiefs agreed to land cessions, they often alienated the more traditional element of their people, who opposed any further loss of ancestral lands. These individuals now had an outlet; Ottawas, Chippewas, Potawatomis, and others broke from the chiefs they felt had betrayed them and set off in search of the Prophet, who preached that the Great Spirit had made the land for Native Americans and not for U.S. citizens. They appreciated his separatist and nativist ideas, and his vision of the future—including the return of the land they had lost—gave them hope. Some made Greenville their home, while others became missionaries, journeying among the native nations and spreading the Prophet's words. Menominees, Miamis, Weas, Delawares, and others became part of the Greenville story. Together, in the initial efforts to build the village, they raised a massive council house, approximately 150 feet long and 34 feet wide, which served for political meetings, as well as an open-air amphitheater for religious gatherings and many dozens of houses. As impressive as the village was, the most remarkable thing about Greenville was how far its message traveled. The Prophet's teachings spread further geographically than any Native American religious teaching that had come before it. Followers of the Prophet's movement appeared as far away as Montana and Florida. Nothing else compared to this phenomenon until Wovoka's Ghost Dance religion in the late 1880s and early 1890s.

The rapid success of his message heartened the Prophet, who enjoyed his new celebrity, but it meant unexpected challenges for Tecumseh, who was responsible for the burgeoning community of Greenville. The number of visitors arriving was staggering. In April 1807 alone, about 400 men, women, and children passed through Fort Wayne en route to Greenville to hear the Prophet speak. Some pilgrims, when told of the Prophet's teachings, left their crops in the field and came without stores or supplies. Tecumseh had to provide for them all. One source of very modest assistance, not to mention peace and goodwill, came from unlikely allies. A group of white settlers established a community at Turtle Creek, Ohio, not far from Greenville. They were not just any settlers, however; they were Shakers, members of a strict religious sect who understood very well what it was like to suffer persecution for their faith and to feel displaced by the mainstream U.S. culture. Rather than fearing the American Indians at Greenville, they sensed a kinship with the sober, industrious, peaceful Native American community. They visited Greenville and even heard the Prophet speak. They reported receiving kind and hospitable treatment and discovering many things to admire about the Prophet's revitalization movement. The Prophet urged his people to abandon their sinful ways, for example, and so, too, did the Shakers. They became Tecumseh's allies, assisting with supplies and food whenever they could.

Tecumseh also looked elsewhere for assistance. Some of the past land cession treaties with the Shawnees stipulated that certain annuities be paid by the United States to the Shawnee leaders for use on behalf of their people. Tecumseh knew from past experience that the Shawnees could not rely on receiving the annuities, despite the fact the payments were part of contracts the United States had made. Even if the annuities were available, it was unclear if officials would apportion some to him. Nonetheless, he approached officials in Ohio, requesting what he believed was his by right. They refused to assign him any of the funds due the Shawnees. He then petitioned Michigan's Governor William Hull, in Detroit. This time he was successful, and he accepted a good portion of the Shawnee annuities on behalf of his community.

Officials in Ohio worried about the fast-growing community of Greenville. The constant stream of American Indians into the area unnerved the settlers nearby. The Prophet did not exactly ease their fears; as his following grew, his teachings became more pointed. He continued to encourage American Indians to separate themselves from whites culturally, economically, and spiritually, but he also went further. He claimed that the Great Spirit had created the American Indians and the British, while an evil spirit created those whites who lived in the United States. He advocated a policy of peace, but his sharpened critique of U.S. citizens was not lost on his audience.

Then, in May 1807, a white man was murdered near Greenville. Tensions rose to a nearly unbearable level. Ohio's Governor Edward Tiffin called a conference the following month to defuse what he feared would become a violent situation. Both Tecumseh and Black Hoof attended with members of their respective communities, and both sides came armed, to the distress of the soldiers of the Ohio militia who were ordered to keep the peace. During a meeting fraught with animosity, Tecumseh's ally Roundhead accused Black Hoof of the murder of the white settler, more for political reasons than from evidence. (In fact, all of the Shawnees were innocent; the murderer was later discovered to be a Potawatomi.) Tecumseh changed the atmosphere of the conference, however, when he addressed the assembled attendees. Accounts from firsthand witnesses agree that he spoke with great passion, energy, and eloquence. One white witness compared his charisma to that of the legendary U.S. orator and statesman Henry Clay. While his style impressed, Tecumseh's speech reflected a great deal about his own agenda.

First, he restored peace to the immediate gathering. He then sought to heal the rift between his followers and Black Hoof's. He publicly separated himself from his brother, criticizing the Prophet's accusations of sorcery against the Wapakoneta chiefs—accusations that could have led to the deaths of Black Hoof and his compatriots—and denouncing the witch-hunts altogether. His address made clear where Tecumseh's loyalties lay. It proved that he was devoted to the pursuit of Shawnee and pan-tribal unity. He supported his brother only when their paths led in the same direction. He was embarrassed by the Prophet's involvement in events he considered to be below a Shawnee warrior, as cowardly as the torture and execution of prisoners. Moreover, he was frustrated by the ways in which the Prophet had exacerbated divisions within Shawnee society, rather than transcending them. Tecumseh was willing to allow his brother to be the focus of attention when it served his own goals, but he was also willing to lose face personally if it meant bringing together his people.

The meeting brought additional honor to Tecumseh, and his reputation as a leader continued to grow. It also underscored the very different natures of the brothers. The Prophet acted from instinct, making plans or statements on a whim, while Tecumseh acted from deliberation, according to a guiding set of goals. Together, the one posed difficulties for the other. At the moment, the Prophet celebrity helped Tecumseh's agenda; the Prophet's prophetic nativism reinforced Tecumseh's political pan-tribalism. But it was not a pattern that could continue indefinitely.

The success of Greenville continued to make onlookers nervous. This was particularly true after June 22, 1807. On that date, the British warship *Leopard* fired on and boarded the U.S. frigate *Chesapeake*. The United States and Great Britain seemed closer than ever to open warfare. This affected policy within the United States. Tecumseh and the Prophet both shared an animosity for William Wells, the Indian Agent at Fort Wayne. Wells reciprocated their feelings. (It is difficult, in fact, to determine who did like Wells, as his superiors seemed as unimpressed with him as the American Indians.) After the *Leopard-Chesapeake* incident, Wells saw the opportunity to link two U.S. fears. He petitioned Secretary of War Henry Dearborn to remove the Prophet from Greenville by force as a threat, claiming that the entire Greenville community had been architected by British agents bent on destroying the United States. Although Wells made a very weak case for his conspiracy theory, William Henry Harrison adopted it. Harrison reported to Washington, D.C., that the Prophet was "an engine set to work by the British for some bad purpose."[2]

Worried that one front of a forthcoming war might be directly on his doorstep, the new governor of Ohio, Thomas Kirker, sent a delegation to Greenville to enquire about the intentions of the Prophet. He received a reply: Greenville would send a delegation to talk to Kirker and other state officials at Chillicothe. Kirker welcomed the delegation, but with wariness. He ordered his militia to mobilize and prepare for battle, just in case. In September 1807, the delegation reached Chillicothe. Its leader was not the Prophet, however, but Tecumseh. He addressed the governor in a meeting that was open to the public and reportedly packed with onlookers. Tecumseh spoke for more than three hours, and his impassioned address marked a turning point in his thought and career.

Tecumseh delivered his points, via interpreter, with care and precision. Past land cession treaties between the United States and his people were illegitimate, he argued, and he presented detailed reasons in each case why this was so. U.S. citizens now occupied the lands in question, however, and he recognized that this effectively rendered moot the question of the treaties' validity. Tecumseh said that his people would not attempt to remove U.S. settlers from these lands, but they likewise would not surrender any lands above the Ohio River. His people did not want war, he explained, but they would show no hesitation in defending their remaining lands with their lives. Previously, Tecumseh had refused to recognize the boundaries drawn by past treaties between the United States and Native America, but now he changed his position, because he hoped that he could use the borders in defense of his people to halt westward expansion, insisting that the United States remain on its side of the line. As impassioned as Tecumseh's speech was, it was also eminently reasonable. Kirker was so impressed by the address that he immediately ordered his troops to stand down.

The success of Tecumseh's presentation was clear in many ways. From the U.S. perspective, he had come to Chillicothe as the Prophet's brother and left as the great orator and defender of his people, Tecumseh. A parallel shift seemed to take place in Greenville. Previously, the community had focused primarily on the religious teachings of the Prophet. Now political concerns seemed to overtake spiritual ones. The people turned their attention to the protection of their remaining lands. Talk of occupying, and thus securing, the last remnants of ancestral homelands replaced speculation about the coming apocalypse and last judgment. The Prophet's separatist teachings certainly complemented such concerns, but Tecumseh's agenda, and not the Prophet's, increasingly captured the community's attention.

Of course, Tecumseh's acceptance of the treaty boundaries meant a tremendous personal sacrifice. Greenville, after all, was located on the U.S. side of the border. He and his brother had to move their entire community. This they did in grand style. They chose a spot below the mouth of the Tippecanoe River in what is today Tippecanoe County, Indiana. The town sprung up almost overnight to include a central council house, a medicine lodge, and approximately 200 houses arranged in lanes, bordered by cultivated fields. The community was a labor of love. Whites dubbed it Prophetstown. Tecumseh missed one of his primary advisers and supporters, however; Blue Jacket, one of the great spirits of the confederacy movement of the 1790s and a firm friend of Tecumseh, chose not to relocate but rather to live out his final days in his Michigan home.

With a new location came new influences. Ironically, although the British had not been the power behind Greenville, they now were looking hard for potential allies while trying not to appear as if they were. Tentative queries reached Prophetstown to gauge the brothers' receptiveness to deeper British friendship. More militant Native Americans involved in a western attempt to forge a warlike confederacy—an effort linked with the Sacs and the Sioux, among others—visited the community and shared their ideas. The most notable new influence was the community's neighbor Main Poc, an infamous Potawatomi war chief and religious leader from Illinois. He, too, was far less interested in peace than either the Prophet or Tecumseh had claimed to be. In fact, he represented the antithesis of the Prophet's teachings. An alcoholic and overt warmonger, he showed little self-control and was known to behave often in a violent and out-of-control fashion. His followers were exceptionally loyal, however. They believed that he possessed special powers and could not be judged as other men; they took the fact he had been born without fingers or a thumb on his left hand as physical proof of his magic. The combined effect was increased militancy, urgency, and energy in the thriving village of Prophetstown.

Tecumseh focused on his political goals: recognizing the common ownership of all remaining American Indian lands by all native nations, so that no group could intentionally or unintentionally dispossess another from its home, and creating a pan-tribal political and military confederacy that would unite all native nations under his leadership. To achieve both goals, Tecumseh had to bridge the intra- and intertribal rifts that stood in the way of Native American cooperation and common action. Prophetstown was fast becoming a self-sufficient success story, but Tecumseh did not tarry to enjoy his accomplishment. He had his own traveling to do, his own kind of missionary work to perform.

NOTES

1. Quoted in Edgar Eggleston and Elizabeth Eggleston Seelye, *Tecumseh and the Shawnee Prophet* (New York: Dodd, Mead, 1878), pp. 118–119.

2. Quoted in John Sudgen, *Tecumseh: A Life* (New York: Henry Holt, 1997), pp. 157–158.

Chapter 5

TECUMSEH'S MESSAGE

Tecumseh journeyed first to Canada to speak to representatives of the British government. The trip had been some time in the making. Canadian officials had invited the Prophet to hold talks with them more than once. The Prophet always sent back congenial replies but never accepted the invitations. Although the British continued to think of the Prophet as the leader in charge of the Prophetstown Shawnees and their multitribal neighbors, both brothers knew that if anyone would travel to represent them and their settlement, it would be Tecumseh. The Prophet acted as a diplomat with non-Natives only reluctantly and in Tecumseh's absence. Yet Tecumseh did not hurry to act on these invitations, either. There were several reasons for Tecumseh to be wary about strengthening ties with Canada. First, he and his people were occupied with relocating from Greenville and establishing Prophetstown, which was no small feat. Second, he had little desire for an awkward encounter in Canada with the Wapakoneta Shawnees, led by Black Hoof and his fellow chiefs, and he knew that the British had invited them for similar talks. Third, Tecumseh did not trust the British; he had not forgotten how he and the other warriors who retreated from the Battle of Fallen Timbers were denied safe haven in Fort Miami by British soldiers, their supposed allies. He recognized that the British were seeking support from the American Indians in case war should break out between Great Britain and the United States, but Tecumseh was reluctant to commit his followers to either side of an Anglo war. His first concern was Native America.

Nevertheless, the British were insistent with their invitations, and Tecumseh decided that at last the time was right. He traveled to Fort Malden in Canada, opposite Detroit in the United States, near Amherstburg. There he met with Superintendent-General William Claus. Also present was Matthew Elliott, a former agent and trader, now Indian superintendent at Amherstburg, who was already known to Tecumseh as a friend. Elliott was Scottish by birth and Shawnee by long habit, language, and marriage. The trio met on June 13, 1808, to discuss the political and military situation. The meeting reflected several things about Tecumseh's strategy. First, Tecumseh was a practical leader; although he did not trust the British and in fact harbored bad feelings about their past treatment of his people, he recognized that he could not alienate them, as he might need them on his side if his movement was to continue. Second, his message was becoming increasingly political in its focus. Unlike the Prophet's religious teachings about the need to remain separate from whites to maintain cultural purism, Tecumseh realized that building his pan-tribal confederacy would require interaction with Anglo governments and working within their system of diplomacy. Third, Tecumseh—although the British still considered him the Prophet's brother at this time—was aware not only of his potential need for an alliance with the British but also of the potential British need for an alliance with him. Speaking not only for his Shawnee followers but also for Native America as a whole, Tecumseh was assuming his place on the world stage.

Claus apparently made it clear that he hoped he could call on Tecumseh for assistance should war break out between Great Britain and the United States. Tecumseh was sympathetic but noncommittal. He was building a pan-tribal union, he explained, to protect American Indian land. He and his people would defend themselves and their property, but they had no wish to court additional hostilities. He had no desire to lead his followers into a white man's war. Tecumseh's eloquence impressed Claus, and the superintendent-general asked Tecumseh to remain and take part in a council with Canadian Lieutenant Governor Francis Gore, who was arriving soon. Tecumseh agreed and spent the interim time visiting Blue Jacket's Shawnee village and nearby Wyandot towns, spreading the message of his confederacy.

When Gore arrived at Fort Malden, officials sent word first to Tecumseh, the leader who had made such an impression on them. They also forwarded Gore's speech so that he might consider it and disseminate it. Tecumseh was aware that the Wyandots considered themselves to be the first people of the region and that they took offense at the fact that the British had contacted Tecumseh before anyone else. Using his diplomatic skill, he helped to smooth over the frustrations caused by this unintentional faux pas and allow the meeting to continue. Gore's address to Tecumseh and the other Native American leaders was a variation on a theme by now familiar to them. He warned them against trusting representatives of the United States and reminded them that Great Britain remained committed to the 1768 boundary between the colonies and American Indian lands. If Great Britain should prevail against the United States in combat with Native American assistance, he implied, that boundary could be restored and many native lands returned to their traditional possessors. To punctuate his words, Gore offered the assembly a detailed and finely crafted belt of wampum. Its artwork depicted Gore and the Americans with a heart in between them, symbolizing their goodwill and unity of purpose.

Tecumseh's appearance at the council was a tremendous success. With his eloquent words and political skill, he gained the respect and attention of the British and the Native Americans in attendance. He left the British—including key leaders such as the lieutenant governor and the superintendent-general—convinced of his abilities and of the momentum behind Prophetstown, and eager to draw closer to him and to woo him as a powerful ally. He likewise impressed the northern chiefs and their representatives. Of all of the leaders in attendance, Tecumseh was chosen to take Gore's wampum belt, show it at Prophetstown, and then be responsible for its circulation among the native nations. Tecumseh had not committed his people to any cause but their own, while he left with great honor and respect. It was a public relations triumph, and he returned like a victor to Prophetstown.

While Tecumseh was convincing the British that he was a leader to be taken seriously, the Prophet was convincing the United States that he was not. During Tecumseh's travels in the north, the Prophet faced a dire situation in Prophetstown. The town was new, and although community members planted fields, the crops were not yet ready to harvest. In the meantime, the recently relocated population needed to eat. Moreover, word of the new town inspired a fresh wave of interest, and visitors came from all directions to learn about the movement Prophetstown represented. The swelling numbers of people exacerbated the food shortage. The Prophet worried that some of the American Indians, pushed to desperation, might begin to steal livestock from the lands of nearby white settlers, and that the situation would ignite in violence. In order to avert such actions before they became widespread, the Prophet felt he had no choice but to request assistance from the territorial governor, William Henry Harrison. The Prophet must have been acutely aware that he was petitioning the very same man who had ridiculed him publicly and tried to turn his people against him (albeit with a rather spectacular lack of success, especially in the case of the eclipse). He did not know, but might have guessed, that Harrison had claimed to his superiors that the Prophet's call for religious revitalization was a scheme devised and implemented by the British.

Certainly, it could not have been easy for the Prophet to meet with Harrison. In August 1808, however, he did. The encounter reflected the Prophet at his most conciliatory and least offensive. He underscored how his religious teachings were helping Native Americans to come together and better themselves and their communities. He stressed how his movement produced the very same results desired by the United States and its civilization campaign: namely the reform and betterment of American Indians. Although his somber and emotional religious pronouncements reportedly affected his Native audiences greatly, the Prophet was neither an orator nor a diplomat. Harrison found him to be rather unimpressive personally, and, because of this, Harrison felt that the Prophet and Prophetstown were less of a threat than he had first believed. By the time the Prophet finished extolling the virtues of his spiritual program, Harrison even believed that the Prophetstown movement might be harnessed as a tool for U.S. purposes. Harrison gave the Prophet the assistance he requested to help feed his people. Ironically, while Harrison was meeting with the Prophet and thinking of Prophetstown's place in U.S. strategy, Tecumseh was receiving gifts from British officials in Canada.

The Prophet's success with Harrison did not mean an end to problems in Prophetstown. When Tecumseh arrived home, he discovered the village reeling from the effects of disease, probably influenza. The number of dead alarmed him and continued to rise. Individuals from various native nations were stricken, but the disease seemed to prey worst upon the Ottawas and the Chippewas. For some reason, their populations were especially vulnerable to the illness. The Ottawa chief Little King died, along with a number of his people. The exact death toll remains uncertain. After Little King's demise, many of the Ottawas and Chippewas who were not infected decided to leave Prophetstown and go back to their homes in Michigan. In fact, they blamed the Prophet for the deaths they had suffered, claiming that he had maliciously poisoned their people. Their misplaced blamed frustrated the brothers, but their departure had its benefits: the remaining food stores of Prophetstown could feed the smaller population that remained through the winter.

Disease and death did not keep others away from Prophetstown for long. Tecumseh gained a particularly stalwart ally in the Potawatomi civil chief Shabeni ("He Has Pawed Through"). Shabeni traveled from his home village at the mouth of the Fox River to visit Prophetstown, and, once he arrived, he became a lifelong convert to Tecumseh's cause. He later joined Tecumseh on some of his other trips to share his message with other native nations. Tecumseh also attracted American Indians from the more militant western nations such as the Sacs, the Foxes, and the Winnebagos. In other cases, Tecumseh had to circumvent the acting chiefs to communicate his message to the warriors of a village; these peoples, however, were already deeply opposed to U.S. expansionism, and their chiefs supported Tecumseh as readily as their people. It seemed that the more disgruntled a group was with the United States, the more its members were interested in the movement based at Prophetstown.

The momentum of these new followers helped to push the Prophetstown community atmosphere in a more warlike direction. The overt hostility they showed toward the United States, as well as the numbers they represented when they visited Prophetstown, helped to fuel rumors of impending violence. White settlers began to panic, fearing to be caught in the midst of war. The Prophet did not help the situation. His rhetoric turned increasingly militant along with his audience. He reportedly preached the need for military as well as religious unity, and some claimed that he encouraged his followers to hoard weapons and ammunition. William Henry Harrison heard the rumors and apparently realized that the Prophet might not be as harmless as he had appeared in person. Harrison ordered two companies of militia to muster and stand by as a precautionary measure. The Prophet tried to convince the new Indian agent at Fort Wayne, John Johnston, that the situation had not changed and that peaceful internal reform was the only priority at Prophetstown, but Harrison was unconvinced. He sent spies posing as traders into Prophetstown to give him eyewitness reports on American Indian rhetoric and actions there.

After a brief pause in Prophetstown, Tecumseh returned to his recruitment tour. Throughout the summer of 1809, he traveled east through Ohio and possibly as far as New York. As his visited various villages and councils, he reiterated his message of pan-tribalism. He warned that U.S. expansionism would continue and that only unity among Native Americans—political and military—would ensure that American Indians could retain possession of their remaining ancestral lands. He urged his listeners to consider these lands as held in common with all American Indians. This meant that all must be represented for any land treaty with the United States to be legitimate. He also invited his audiences to visit Prophetstown, perhaps even relocate their homes there, and join with him in his new confederacy. At every stop, Tecumseh emphasized the urgency of his mission.

Although Tecumseh called for unity, his words tended to have a rather schismatic effect on the villages he visited. Chiefs and elders often questioned the urgency of Tecumseh's plea. After all, they had already endured many land cession treaties. Some of these leaders had been complicit in them, in fact, and now worked closely with missionaries, government representatives, and other whites in undertaking "civilizing" projects for their people. Their focus on changing local economies and lifestyles made them sluggish in thinking beyond their village to the larger problems of Native America as a whole. Moreover, others suspected that the leaders of the United States were more preoccupied with possible hostilities with Great Britain than with negotiating further land cessions.

The younger American Indians—especially the warriors, whose position in their society seemed to be endangered—disagreed. Many thought their leaders had lost credibility and authority by acquiescing in past land cession treaties. Others resented attempts to remake their culture after the model of Anglo agricultural life, effectively defining their traditional roles as fighters and hunters out of existence. Tecumseh found ready recruits among these younger individuals. Still more were deeply sympathetic to and interested in his message but unwilling to follow him immediately. These warriors hung in the balance, thinking over what they had heard, waiting to see what developed. They required only a small push to join Tecumseh's movement. They soon had it.

Nothing, however, was inevitable. The summer of 1809 was a crucial moment in relations between the United States and Native America. U.S. leaders might have averted future bloodshed if they had listened to the complaints brought to them, calmed frustration with compromise, followed their own laws and treaties, considered the impact of their policies and decisions, and refused to fuel the militant unrest of the growing resistance movement. For example, the U.S. Embargo Act of 1807 and, more important, the Non-Intercourse of 1809 blocked trade with the British and the French. These laws had a negative effect on the U.S. economy, but they imposed a greater hardship on American Indians. Relocated or barred from their traditional hunting and farming lands, Native Americans relied heavily on British and French traders for food, as well as other supplies for daily living. This situation was one of many that might have been assuaged and not exacerbated if U.S. leaders had followed different courses of action. It would have been in the interest of the United States as well as of Native America to reach some sort of conciliation, because the United States appeared to be headed for formal war with Great Britain and needed allies on the American continent. At this crucial time, however, William Henry Harrison, governor of Indiana Territory, did not seek alliance or understanding with the native nations. Instead, he did the one thing that Tecumseh had both predicted and feared: he pushed for another land cession treaty.

Tecumseh brought his message to Wapakoneta, the home of the rival Shawnee chief Black Hoof. Black Hoof and his fellow leaders refused to listen to his talk, but some of the village warriors showed great interest. Tecumseh's long-time friend, the "white Indian" Stephen Ruddell, attended his address. While Tecumseh was there, Ruddell interpreted a letter from Governor Harrison to the chiefs. What Tecumseh heard made him so furious that he took the letter from Ruddell and threw it in the council fire. If Harrison had been there, Tecumseh claimed, he would have done the same to him. By pressing for additional land from the native nations, Harrison vindicated Tecumseh and his urgent warnings. He also provided those warriors who hung in the balance the motivation they needed to join Tecumseh's movement actively. It was a point of no return for relations between the United States and Native America.

Harrison had personal reasons for pursuing his agenda. Despite the fact that a call for additional land cessions only heightened American Indian frustrations and risked pushing the native nations toward alliance with the British, Harrison pushed forward for regional political and economic reasons. Harrison was building his reputation and career in Indiana Territory primarily by shepherding the land toward statehood. Early in 1809, however, the United States divided the region, and a portion of it became Illinois Territory. The loss of Illinois, specifically the population of Illinois, was a blow to Harrison and a major setback for his plans for Indiana statehood. He needed more settlers in order to make a bid for statehood; of course, he needed more rich lands in order to attract more settlers. Moving the native population away from the fertile Wabash River lands, Harrison decided, would be the best way to achieve his goals. As before, Harrison did not prove to be particularly worried about what means he used to accomplish his task.

When Harrison asked permission from the new U.S. president, James Madison, to negotiate this land purchase, he identified two tracts of land that he wished to obtain for his territory. When he went before the representatives of the American Indians, however, he asked for three tracts of land. The third, the one he did not disclose to Madison, closed more than half of the distance between Harrison in Vincennes and Tecumseh and the Prophet in Prophetstown and moved beyond the boundary set by the Treaty of Greenville. Unaware of this third tract, Madison gave his blessing to the negotiations on three conditions. First, the price paid for lands had to be consistent with earlier prices given for similar property in comparable treaties. Second, all Native Americans who were owners—or who claimed to be owners—of the lands in questions had to be represented at the treaty talks. Third, Harrison had to make certain that the land cession "will excite no disagreeable apprehensions, and produce no undesirable effects."[1] Of the three conditions, Harrison met only one: he paid a bit less than two cents for each acre of land, a sum similar to that paid for previous land cessions.

As for the other two conditions, Harrison actively violated them. The proceedings were farcical. Harrison brought large numbers of starving, suffering Potawatomis from Michigan and the St. Joseph River to the talks, despite the fact that they had no claim to the lands in question. Their terrible plight made them desperate for help from any direction, and Harrison promised assistance if they could convince their peers to surrender their lands. The Potawatomis became a perpetual chorus at the negotiations in favor of the treaty, a lever used against their fellow native nations. While the Potawatomis were well represented, the only people who were actually living on the land in question at the time were not present. The Weas had the right, according to Harrison's 1805 treaty, to decide what happened to these particular lands, along with their neighbors the Miamis and the Eel Rivers. The Weas, however, were absent from the negotiations. Later, when the agreement was effectively concluded, representatives of the Weas finally succumbed to pressure to agree to the treaty. The people who hunted on the property—including Kickapoos, Piankeshaws, and Tecumseh's Shawnees—were not consulted at all.

Harrison led those who did attend to agree to the treaty by a series of threats and promises. One pledge he made, for example, was that the United States would seek no more land cessions in the region. In less than two years, this would be proved false. Not only were Harrison's tactics not approved by Washington, D.C., but they also were worrisome to his fellow officials in Indiana. His staff members and other witnesses debated going over his head and reporting his behavior to higher authorities, perhaps even President Madison. Nevertheless, both sides signed the Treaty of Fort Wayne, on September 20, 1809. More than three million acres of land became part of Indiana Territory. This massive transfer of lands marked a turning point. Even those nations that had supported the United States historically, such as the Miamis, recognized the Treaty of Fort Wayne as one U.S. step too far into Native America. They turned from their traditional alliance with the United States into the arms of Tecumseh's pan-tribal resistance movement.

In response to the Treaty of Fort Wayne, Tecumseh adopted an even bolder message. To protect their remaining lands, he said, American

Indians had to cooperate. They had a vested interest now in all of the territories still claimed by native nations; they should consider these lands to be held in common. No land cession treaties were valid without the consent of all. In effect, he dismissed all agreements after the Treaty of Greenville as illegitimate—including, and most especially, the Treaty of Fort Wayne. Protesting these invalid treaties had to become a way of life. One of the best ways to do this, he said, was to refuse to accept the U.S. annuities tied to these agreements. He knew that he was asking a tremendous sacrifice of his people, but he believed that refusing U.S. payments allowed the Native Americans to maintain the high moral ground and to be consistent and unified in their policy toward what he considered to be a hostile U.S. government. This new form of protest marked a substantial change in Tecumseh's thinking, as he himself had accepted annuities on behalf of his people previously. But that was before the Treaty of Fort Wayne.

To promote his message of unity, Tecumseh was willing to challenge the very structure of the native nations he hoped to recruit into his confederacy. He knew that many chiefs would not be willing to reject U.S. payments for past land cessions; for some, receiving and distributing the annuities was one of their primary sources of ongoing authority among their people. The annuities had convinced a good number of the leaders to agree to treaties in the first place, and so giving up the payments meant admitting the gravity of their mistakes. For that matter, many chiefs still found it difficult to follow Tecumseh or to accept his idea of a pan-tribal union, because that meant subordinating their own positions beneath his leadership. Tecumseh considered these leaders unworthy. He bypassed their authority by appealing directly to their warriors, and the warriors responded. For people such as the Winnebagos, this led to massive shifts in the traditional hierarchy of their society.

Tecumseh and the Prophet sent out word in all directions that they were hosting an intertribal conference in the summer of 1810 to discuss the situation between the native nations and the United States. By spring, approximately one thousand American Indians had descended upon Prophetstown. Although the brothers attempted to be clandestine when spreading the message of the meeting, they found it impossible to keep such large numbers of visitors a secret. Whites in surrounding settlements watched and worried. As Prophetstown continued to draw newcomers, Tecumseh made a special trip to the villages on the Detroit River, and particularly to the Wyandot village of Brownstown. This community was symbolically important to Tecumseh and his movement, because it was the seat of the Northwest Confederacy from 1786 through 1795. Brownstown epitomized the kind of pan-tribal unity Tecumseh wished to inspire in his contemporaries. He hoped both to invoke the spirit and transcend the accomplishments of that earlier union. He was successful in his trip, and representatives returned with him to Prophetstown, bringing with them an old wampum belt that represented the earlier confederacy. Their actions proved that they recognized Tecumseh as the inheritor of Joseph Brant's tradition of unified resistance.

When Tecumseh returned to Prophetstown, he had the opportunity to practice the kind of resistance that he preached. He interrupted French boatmen unloading salt annuities that the United States owed to the Shawnees and Kickapoos according to treaty. Tecumseh refused to accept them and insisted that they be returned. The workers complied and took back the salt. They reported their encounter with the passionate leader as a frightening one.

The intertribal council met in May 1810. Tecumseh and the Prophet were wary of the attention the gathering had drawn and of the U.S. spies they knew to be in Prophetstown, and so they held the meeting in the more secluded location of Parc-aux-Vaches. Although the various leaders recognized how close they were to conflict, they could not agree on going to war with the United States immediately. The consensus was that the short-term solution might include waiting, preparing, and, if possible, negotiating. This plan was soon put to the test as violence flared. A series of small, isolated events—horse and cattle thefts, random shootings—involved various individuals (including Kickapoos and Creeks) who could be traced to Prophetstown. These events were not planned by either Tecumseh or the Prophet. But, with so many visitors moving through the town, it was unsurprising that a few of might be linked to criminal acts. In response to these events, Harrison sent a message to the Prophet, who, he believed, was the sole leader in charge of Prophetstown.

Harrison's message was blunt—and not altogether sincere. He praised the Prophetstown warriors as brave, but warned that his militia warriors were equally so, and that he had the greater numbers. He pointed out that his warriors outnumbered the British warriors, as well, so the Prophet would be misguided to look to the British for assistance. He offered to hear complaints about treaties and suggested that he might be willing to return lands if they had been wrongly sold. He also offered to help the Prophet make his case to President Madison himself, if he wished to do so. Harrison's messenger, Joseph Barron, took the message to Prophetstown, but it was Tecumseh and not the Prophet who responded to it. Tecumseh's reply was equally straightforward. He did not desire war with the United States, he explained, but he also could not stand by idly while his people were robbed. The American Indians owned the land together, in common, and the United States could not arbitrarily divide it up in order to purchase it from only a few of them. He, Tecumseh, accepted Harrison's invitation to talk. He would come to Vincennes to meet with Harrison. He would bring thirty chosen men, but more undoubtedly would choose to accompany him.

Harrison was bemused by the reply. He responded, saying that only the chiefs and a few escorts were welcome in Vincennes. It seemed that he realized too late his errors. First, he worried that the Native Americans would arrive under the auspices of peaceful talks only to attack and launch a war. Second, he recognized that he had misunderstood who was really in control of Prophetstown. In a letter to the U.S. secretary of war, he identified Tecumseh as the driving force behind the Prophetstown movement with a combination of admiration and fear: "This brother," he wrote, "is really the efficient man—the Moses of the family...described by all as a bold, active, sensible man, daring in the extreme, and capable of any undertaking."[2] Tecumseh did not intend to attack Harrison and launch a war with the United States. He also did not intend to limit his number of escorts to Vincennes. He arrived accompanied by 75 American Indians of various native nations. On August 15, 1810, Tecumseh—or "the Prophet's brother," as many of the white settlers continued to call him—went to Grouseland, the home of the territorial governor, to meet William Henry Harrison face to face for the first time.

This first encounter between Tecumseh and Harrison became the subject of legend. Eyewitness reports suggest that one widely reported story, at least, probably is true; Harrison sat on a raised platform erected on the grounds, surrounded by his staff and soldiers, facing the warriors who came with Tecumseh. When Tecumseh approached, Harrison offered him a seat on the dais. Tecumseh refused, however, saying the earth was the best place for an Indian, because his people preferred to rest on the bosom of their mother. He then sat on the ground. This simple gesture inverted the power dynamic of the meeting—the man on the high stage was not the one in control—and stunned the assembled crowd into silence. It also made a symbolic point about Tecumseh's connection to and conviction about the land. Most of Harrison's experience with American Indians had been related to negotiations for treaties or petitions for assistance. Tecumseh approached Harrison with neither fear nor need, neither threats nor requests. Harrison realized that Tecumseh was unlike any other Native American leader he had ever met.

Tecumseh's presentation also differed from any other Harrison had ever heard. Tecumseh claimed to represent all of Native America. He did not deny the fact he was building a pan-tribal confederacy to protect American Indian land. He emphasized a key point: he and his people desired only opportunity, not charity. They demanded justice. He catalogued wrongs committed against his people—specifically, the land cession treaties he considered to be illegitimate—and asked for these injustices to be reversed. He and his followers did not want war, Tecumseh said, but they would fight to protect what was theirs. It took several days for him to make his case thoroughly. Throughout his comments, the atmosphere remained tense.

As he spoke, Tecumseh offered a long-ranging historical account of his people's interactions with representatives of Europe and the United States. The French, he claimed, were the best white neighbors, because they gave gifts, initiated trade, and otherwise asked for and interfered with little. The British, he said, used his people to fight their wars for their purposes and gain. They did not, however, take Native American land, he asserted. (Clearly, Tecumseh was not above exaggerating his point for dramatic effect, because he knew this was not a completely accurate representation of the land policies of the "Long Knives.") In contrast to the French and British, he said, the United States acted repeatedly in an exploitative manner toward American Indians. His list of U.S. acts of bad faith was long and punctuated by specific, detailed illustrations: killing Moluntha despite his acquiescence to the U.S. treaty; forcing Native Americans into wars; stealing American Indian property, dividing the native nations and forcing individual groups into selling land; and leaving American Indians no choice but to do violence in order to protect themselves and their possessions. He even went so far as to implicate the United States in the smallpox and other disease epidemics that had plagued his people—a charge related to suspicions he had voiced in the past about U.S. annuities possibly being tainted for the purpose of infecting the native recipients.

Then came the heart of Tecumseh's message to Harrison and the United States. He explained that the native nations held their lands in common and that the United States had to deal with them accordingly when arranging for the purchase of any lands. The past treaties that were unfairly negotiated were illegitimate, and American Indians would not recognize their validity. He was bold and unapologetic, not to mention shockingly honest, about his plans: he was circumventing those chiefs who acted essentially as pawns of the U.S. government and appealing directly to their warriors, who were assuming the powers and responsibilities these leaders had abdicated. Those who had allowed land cessions would be held accountable, and if any bloodshed resulted, the guilt rested on the United

States. Under his guidance, the native nations would unite and stand firm against further surrender of native lands. Harrison, Tecumseh explained, had a choice. He could avoid conflict by returning the land taken via illegitimate treaties and allow Native Americans to trade freely, or he could choose war. Tecumseh and his followers had no wish for U.S. annuities or assistance; they desired only to own their land and to trade with those who wished to trade with them, in order to provide for themselves. He left the decision in Harrison's hands.

The days Tecumseh had spent outlining and justifying his position yielded nothing. Harrison knew that agreeing to Tecumseh's demands would undo all he had accomplished in the name of Indiana statehood—and, for that matter, his own political career. He responded simply by denying Tecumseh's assertions that the United States had acted unjustly toward his people. Harrison furthermore rejected the idea that the native nations held their land in common and had the right to negotiate collectively about any land cession. There was no room for compromise. This flat refusal incensed Tecumseh to the point that he lost his legendary calm. As Harrison spoke, denying the truth of Tecumseh's claims, Tecumseh stood. His warriors follow suit. Tecumseh gestured angrily and called Harrison a liar. Harrison drew his sword, and his soldiers gathered around him defensively. The talks had reached an impasse. Harrison declared that the council was over and left to put his militia on high alert.

On the next day, an embarrassed Tecumseh apologized for his show of temper, and talks resumed, with wariness apparent on both sides. The exchange was uncomfortable. Tecumseh noted that he had reason to believe that Harrison's behavior with regard to the Treaty of Fort Wayne did not necessarily represent the position and policy of United States. Harrison denied this. Harrison asked if his people could deliver the annuities due the Shawnees by treaty. Tecumseh replied that his people did not want annuities, but instead they wanted their lands. He continued, saying that if the militia tried to take the lands along the Wabash River as provided by the Treaty of Fort Wayne, violence would result and be solely the fault of the United States. Tecumseh finished his statement and retreated. Other Native American leaders representing the Wyandots, Kickapoos, Potawatomis, and Winnebagos spoke in turn, confirming that Tecumseh represented them and that they stood by his message. The meeting ended in a stalemate, with Harrison supporting the Treaty of Fort Wayne and Tecumseh warning of the consequences of its enforcement.

According to Moses Dawson, who both worked with Harrison and later penned his biography, Harrison met once more, privately, with Tecumseh, on August 22. Dawson's retelling of the meeting suggests that Tecumseh had no illusions about his position. Tecumseh told Harrison that he knew the British did not support his movement but hoped only to persuade the American Indians to fight for them in any forthcoming conflict with the United States. Nonetheless, Tecumseh believed that his people would, in the end, be forced into hostilities. If they did enter a war against the United States, Tecumseh said, he would do everything possible to spare women and children. Harrison said he would communicate Tecumseh's message to President Madison but that he doubted this would change the current situation. Tecumseh agreed, noting that the president had the luxury of being far away and would not have to take part when he and Harrison fought the conflict through to its finish. The Tecumseh that emerges from Dawson's account was less an enthusiastic idealist, eager for action, than a realist committed to his cause despite tremendous odds.

After meeting with Harrison, Tecumseh threw himself back into the project of building his confederacy. To meet his goal, he had to overcome multiple obstacles. First, the people he hoped to unify were spread across a wide geographic space. His prospective recruits lived far apart, from the Great Lakes region at the borders of Canada all the way south to Florida and across the vast expanse of the Midwest. These far-flung peoples had other claims on their attention, as well. Tecumseh's message had to compete with immediate concerns from disease and food shortages to internal politics and local allegiances. Furthermore, long-standing intertribal conflicts threatened any idea of unity. For example, two of Tecumseh's strongest supporters, the Illinois Kickapoos and the Rock River Winnebagos, reached a point of open warfare in the summer of 1810, as the Kickapoos organized a raid in revenge for a previous Winnebago slaughter of a Kickapoo group. Both peoples claimed to be committed to Tecumseh's vision of collective resistance, but they could not achieve a lasting peace with each other, much less with other members of a vast, pan-tribal confederacy. Such challenges were exacerbated by language barriers. Creating meaningful unity among groups that literally could not speak to one another was a particular challenge.

Tecumseh's project had certain advantages, however, to balance its obstacles. First, Tecumseh was working within a preexisting tradition of pan-tribalism. Pontiac, Joseph Brant, Blue Jacket, and others had laid the foundation for his movement and the ideas that informed it, including the concept of common Native American ownership of land. Tecumseh possessed an added benefit that his predecessors did not enjoy: he had the Prophet and the prophetic tradition he represented, and this religious ingredient added to the potency of Tecumseh's message. He could claim the moral high ground and the cause of justice; when he needed to do so, he could also claim the direct support of the Great Spirit. Although his potential followers spoke many tongues, Tecumseh's own Shawnee language was widely known and understood, and trade had helped to encourage villages to cultivate interpreters. Additionally, other forms of symbolic speech developed to assist communication, such as the wampum belts with recognizable images that conveyed ideas such as unity, alliance, and war.

Tecumseh was shrewd enough to realize that he did not necessarily need to win over to his movement the native nations as a whole with their established leadership hierarchies. Instead, he needed to convince individuals to follow him. His message was well received by warriors frustrated by compromise and concession who wished to displace chiefs they believed to be ineffective. The decentralization of most native communities meant that these people could easily relocate and reestablish their communities—in other words, they could vote for Tecumseh with their feet. Moreover, Tecumseh's project was timely. The Treaty of Fort Wayne alerted many to the urgency of their situation. So, too, did frequent reminders of the imminent crisis between the United States and Great Britain, a conflict in which Native America inevitably would become entangled.

Following his confrontation with Harrison, Tecumseh returned to his recruitment tour. He tried to keep his movements secret, and he did a very good job; historians today find it difficult to reconstruct his travels during that time and rely heavily on stories and memories shared by witnesses long after the fact. In the summer of 1810, after his meeting in Vincennes, Tecumseh apparently headed west to share his message with native nations more militant than those in the East and vehemently opposed to the United States. He probably visited groups such as the western Potawatomis in villages such as those led by Main Poc, Moquongo, and Little Chief. He stopped in Shabeni's hometown, and the chief joined him for the next leg of his journey. It seems he went down the Illinois River to meet with other Potawatomis there and then followed the Rock River up into Wisconsin to visit villages belonging to the Winnebagos and Menominees. It appears that he met mixed success, especially among the latter peoples. The Menominee chief Tomah reportedly made a stirring speech to his people in which he expressed his desire not to seek bloodshed. He gave his warriors his consent to go to make war, but he would remain on the path of peace. His words swayed many in his audience.

Next, Tecumseh apparently traveled along the Mississippi River in order to meet with members of many native nations who had gathered at key trading locations along that waterway. He also spoke with the Sacs and the Foxes. The Sacs were less than enthusiastic, because they were preoccupied with rejuvenating their economy with new work in local lead mines. Later, the Sac chief Black Hawk recalled the warnings of Tecumseh and the Prophet and admitted that their direst predictions about U.S. expansionism had come true. Tecumseh remained tireless, and next, it seems, he visited with the Missouri Shawnees and their neighbors, the Delawares. Among these people, he discovered two ominous crises. First, they were engaged in deadly witch-hunts. It is unclear how many so-called witches were executed during this scare, but the number may be as high as fifty. The people blamed witchcraft for the spread of disease through the area's villages; there may also have been a political dimension to the witch-hunts, with the accusations and executions serving as a political purge of sorts. Tecumseh vocally opposed the executions and proved instrumental in ending the witch-hunts.

The second crisis involved a pending war with the Shawnees' long-standing enemies the Osages. Tecumseh objected to this intertribal warfare and pleaded for peace. It was a personal test for Tecumseh, and it proved what sacrifices he was willing to make for his movement. The latest hostile incident between the groups involved the killing by some Osages of two Shawnees and one Delaware. One of the victims was a relative of Tecumseh. According to traditional understandings of law and honor, Tecumseh was bound to seek retribution for his kin's death. Instead, he put the cause of pan-tribal unity ahead of his family duty and exhorted all sides to reconcile. His efforts bought time for a trader, with assistance from the Indian agent in St. Louis, to broker a short-term peace among the Osages, the Delawares, and the Shawnees. Tecumseh helped to avert needless bloodshed, but he failed to bring the Shawnees fully on board with his agenda. He probably returned to Prophetstown by way of the home of the Illinois River Kickapoos, who were some of his very first allies.

While Tecumseh was experiencing a mixed reception on his rather unsatisfying tour, his situation had changed for the worse. Approximately two thousand American Indians from nations that had once made up the old Northwest Confederacy met in Brownstown in September. Represented among them were the Ohio Shawnees. The resulting council agreed to a policy of neutrality if the United States and Great Britain declared war. The members also condemned Tecumseh's confederacy outright and claimed that any intertribal union belonged not at Prophetstown but at Brownstone. The news was a blow to Tecumseh. It was not, however, wholly unexpected, even considering the fact that some of those who took part in the meeting had considered themselves sympathetic to

Tecumseh previously. After all, Tecumseh had instigated something of a revolution in many communities, appealing to the warriors and bypassing the chiefs. These undermined leaders now struck back at him, protecting their own positions of power. Furthermore, Tecumseh's message had not changed, but the weather had. It took less resolve in the summer to agree to reject U.S. money and provisions associated with land cession treaties, but when the weather grew cold and the people faced starvation and exposure, many leaders found it difficult to continue to refuse U.S. annuities. By the end of the year, even some of those who originally rejected the annuities—the Weas and the Kickapoos, for example—had admitted defeat and petitioned for the assistance. Removed from their homelands and barred from their hunting grounds, communities recognized their dependence on U.S. assistance. They declared neutrality because they dared not make war on their last source of food and supplies.

It is, perhaps, remarkable that others held out and continued their protest of the treaties, Tecumseh's Shawnees and the western Potawatomis, for example, remained consistent in their refusal of the annuities. Tecumseh realized that he and his followers could not stand alone. Even if all of Native America were unified, its people still needed an ally. After all, American Indians in the Great Lakes region were now outnumbered by whites almost four to one. After a brief stop in Prophetstown, he left for Fort Malden to talk to the British. A group of 150 men, women, and children from the Shawnee, Potawatomi, Ottawa, Winnebago, and Sac nations accompanied him on his journey. It was a grim Tecumseh who met the British officials in Canada. Only two years before, Tecumseh had told these same people that he did not wish to take sides in a white man's conflict and that he hoped a pan-tribal confederacy would be capable of halting peacefully U.S. expansionism into Native American land. Now, after the Treaty of Fort Malden, the meeting with Harrison, and the decision of the Brownstown conference, Tecumseh returned, offering alliance and asking for British help in fighting a war against the United States.

In November 1810, Tecumseh showed officials the old wampum belt depicting the friendship between the British and the American Indians. He claimed that he represented the warriors of Native America, who now controlled the native nations. By next autumn, he said, his confederacy would be complete. Now he claimed the promise of British alliance that was depicted in the wampum belt. Canadian Governor Sir James Craig feared that the United States would blame the British for any Native American hostilities, and he alerted London to the fact that the American Indians were planning war. British officials wondered how to secure Tecumseh and his followers as allies without being pulled into their conflict. The official position was somewhat cynical, if practical; the British wanted to be friends with the native nations when the British needed allies, but they also did not want to risk valuable political or military capital for the sake of the American Indian cause.

The point was moot. Great Britain by itself was headed directly for war with the United States. This suited Tecumseh's plans perfectly.

NOTES

1. Quoted in John Sudgen, *Tecumseh: A Life* (New York: Henry Holt, 1997), p. 183.

2. Ibid., p. 198.

This sketch by Pierre Le Dru shows Tecumseh in a turban with an eagle feather, in traditional Shawnee style, while also wearing a large medallion of George the Third and a British officer's coat, as he might have done on formal occasions with his British allies during the War of 1812. National Anthropological Archives, Smithsonian Institution (gn_00770).

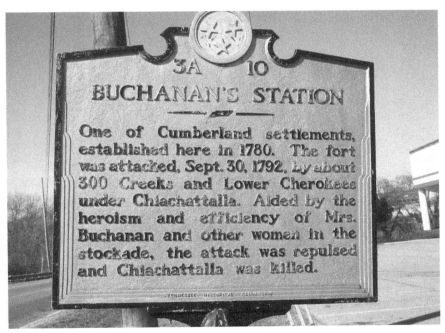

Although the contemporary historical marker does not mention this, Tecumseh participated in the raid at Buchanan's Station while following his elder brother, Cheeseekau ("Shawnee Warrior"), who was killed during the fighting there. Photo by Amy H. Sturgis.

Tecumseh's younger brother Lalawéthika, who became the religious leader known as Tenskwatawa, or the Prophet, alternately helped and hindered Tecumseh's cause of pan-tribal resistance. Smithsonian American Art Museum, Gift of Mrs. Joseph Harrison, Jr.

As governor of Indiana Territory and commander of the Army of the Northwest during the War of 1812, William Henry Harrison proved to be a key obstacle to Tecumseh's dreams for Native America. Courtesy of Library of Congress.

The Battle of Tippecanoe in 1811 was technically a victory for William Henry Harrison's forces, who destroyed Tecumseh's home base of Prophetstown and defeated the warriors defending it, but the battle ultimately failed to achieve Harrison's goals and led to increased bloodshed on the frontier. Courtesy of Library of Congress.

Shawnee chief Black Hoof opposed Tecumseh and his pan-tribal resistance movement and instead advocated cultural adaptation for his people and alliance with the United States. Courtesy of Library of Congress.

DEATH OF WILLIAM HENRY HARRISON.

Born 9th Feb. 1773   Inaugurated President of the United States March 4th 1841   Died 4th April 1841

The death of William Henry Harrison, after the briefest U.S. presidency in the history of the office, helped to fuel the legend of "Tecumseh's curse." Courtesy of Library of Congress.

This bust on the grounds of the U.S. Naval Academy at Annapolis originally was meant to represent the Delaware chief Tamanend, but over time it officially has become identified as a tribute to Tecumseh. Courtesy of Library of Congress.

Tecumseh's death at the Battle of the Thames was immediately romanticized by authors, orators, and artists, as this picture by Currier and Ives illustrates. Courtesy of Library of Congress.

Chapter 6

THE END OF PROPHETSTOWN

Tecumseh redoubled his efforts to recruit American Indian supporters to his confederacy. He revisited villages where he had already delivered his message in an effort to renew support, maintain morale, and control the damage done by the Brownstown council. He planned to begin a new tour in the south. There he had a ready-made audience in Tuckabatchee. Big Warrior, the most powerful chief of the Creek nation, was organizing a southern confederacy based in Tuckabatchee and composed of representatives of many of the southern native nations. Not only was a multitribal presence already assembled there, but Tecumseh knew that these Native Americans were likely to be receptive to his movement, since they were uniting in order to resist U.S. expansionism in their region. Tecumseh believed he would gain many followers in the south.

He was not the only one campaigning for his cause. Others passed a wampum belt among the villages on the Mississippi and Missouri Rivers in order to call for unity and to encourage others to join Tecumseh's movement. Tecumseh's wild ally Main Poc conducted his own journey among the Sacs, Foxes, Potawatomis, Kickapoos, and Dakotas in order to publicize the confederacy. He even went to the British at Fort Malden to reiterate Tecumseh's position. He reported that the native nations had in fact joined together and that the warriors had deposed their chiefs. Native America, he claimed, was ready for war.

Before heading south, Tecumseh retraced his steps in the east, stopping in Wynadot and Seneca villages before making one last attempt to change the minds of the Wapakoneta Shawnees. He had little luck winning Black Hoof and his followers over to the side of pan-tribal resistance. He made better headway with the Wyandots and Senecas on the Sandusky River, however. Some of their people already had relocated to the Wabash River in support of Prophetstown, but now others decided to follow them, and still more committed to relocating within the next two years. Although he did not win over all, or even most, of these villages, Tecumseh gained new followers, and even some of the chiefs proved to be sympathetic to his mission. He left the Wyandots and Senecas with the idea that the seeds he had planted among them would continue to bear fruit.

Following these travels, Tecumseh returned to Prophetstown. He arrived to find that the Prophet had not refused the salt annuities provided by the United States—in fact, he had taken more than the amount to which he was entitled by treaty. Apparently this gave the Prophet the opportunity to brag about how many new followers he expected to be following Tecumseh home from his journey. Clearly, the Prophet had done exactly what Tecumseh had asked others not to do. The Prophet would display increasingly poor judgment in the days to follow, to Tecumseh's disappointment and frustration. Further complicating the Prophetstown situation, William Henry Harrison assigned a new spy to infiltrate the settlement and report back to Vincennes with all he saw and heard. Not only was the Prophet making mistakes—at least from Tecumseh's perspective—but they were closely watched.

Nevertheless, Tecumseh did not think he could afford to remain in Prophetstown and oversee the village's daily affairs. He prepared a delegation led by his Mingo supporters to visit the Six Nations of the Iroquois Confederacy and invite them to take part in the movement. The Mingoes were particularly well suited to share Tecumseh's message in New York, as the Mingo nation had once been a part of the Iroquois Confederacy and continued to share much in common with the Senecas, Cayugas, Oneidas, Mohawks, Onondagas, and Tuscaroras. This mission eventually met great success. Many warriors followed immediately, while others committed to relocating soon. The primary dissent came from an expected source, the chiefs who received U.S. annuities and had no intention of cutting off one of their primary source of power and prestige. As they did elsewhere, the warriors bypassed these leaders in order to rally around the promise of Prophetstown.

Before Tecumseh could depart for the south, Harrison detained him. The reason Harrison used for calling on Tecumseh was that he believed only the Shawnee leader could help restore peace after several violent events shook the frontier. A war scare broke out in Missouri in May 1811 after an American Indian spoke "fighting words" about his people waging war against white settlers. In the following month, two random killings occurred: Menominees killed one or two white men on the Mississippi River, and Potawatomis killed one white man and kidnapped a white woman in Illinois territory. These three events combined led to panic among white settlers, who feared they would be murdered by American Indians, and also among Native Americans, who feared blind retribution from whites. The situation in Illinois was particularly tense. The new territorial governor, Ninian Edwards, demanded that the Potawatomis surrender the guilty parties or face war. The chiefs, who were known before this time to cooperate with the United States, replied that they had little control over their warriors; furthermore, if the governor continued to threaten war, their people might be forced to oblige him and fight.

Harrison's stated cause for contacting Tecumseh, then, was to ask the leader to assist in restoring peace. But Harrison had more than one motivation for summoning the Shawnee chief. After realizing that it was Tecumseh, and not the Prophet, who was the true power behind Prophetstown and the pan-tribal resistance movement, Harrison had followed the chief's actions as closely as possible. He wanted no obstacle to his plans. Even after the Treaty of Fort Wayne, Harrison asked for approval to pursue more land purchases. Other U.S. officials in the area disagreed with him, thinking that in time a combination of poverty and diminishing game would persuade the American Indians to leave their lands willingly. Harrison was impatient, however. He felt that Indiana's potential was badly wasted as long as it remained a territory and frontier—and, no doubt, that his own potential was wasted as long as he remained merely a territorial governor. He saw Tecumseh as a threat to the U.S. statehood for which he had labored for years. Increasingly frustrated by restraints from his superiors—he was denied permission to continue with additional land purchases or, for that matter, even to survey the Fort Wayne purchase or to build a new post on its lands—Harrison looked to strike at the one opponent closest to home.

Harrison was not without genuine admiration for his Shawnee rival, however. In 1811, Harrison wrote what is perhaps the most famous surviving description of Tecumseh:

> The implicit obedience and respect which the followers of Tecumseh pay to him is really astonishing, and more than any other circumstance bespeaks him one of those uncommon geniuses which spring up occasionally to produce revolutions and overturn the established order of things. If it were not for the vicinity of the United States, he would, perhaps, be the founder of an empire that would rival in glory that of Mexico

or Peru. No difficulties deter him. His activity and industry supply the want of letters. For four years he has been in constant motion. You see him today on the Wabash and in a short time you hear of him on the shores of Lake Erie or Michigan. Or on the banks of the Mississippi, and wherever he goes he makes an impression favorable to his purposes.[1]

In his letter to Tecumseh, Harrison asked the Shawnee chief to convince the people of Vincennes that war was not imminent. The recent violence on the frontier had rattled many nerves, he implied, but Tecumseh also was to blame. The territorial governor accused Tecumseh of planning war and, quite possibly, Harrison's own assassination, although he could cite only vague rumors supposedly heard along the Mississippi River as evidence. Harrison also accused the Prophet of stealing salt annuities. He invited Tecumseh to come to Vincennes on two conditions: Tecumseh would bring only a few men, and they would discuss the Treaty of Fort Wayne no further. If Tecumseh and his brother wished to talk directly to President Madison, Harrison would make certain they were able to do so and return safely.

Harrison was in contact with Washington, D.C., but not about orchestrating a possible trip for Tecumseh and the Prophet. The territorial governor was tired of waiting for action. He requested additional military forces from the secretary of war and received them. The president's position was clear: Madison wanted peace, not war, and Harrison should use force only as a last resort if the American Indians attacked. The troops should serve the purpose of self-defense only. Harrison planned to treat these orders, much like those given him for the Treaty of Fort Wayne negotiations, merely as suggestions.

Tecumseh received Harrison's letter on July 3, 1811, and replied the following day, accepting Harrison's offer to speak with him in Vincennes. Although speaking to President Madison undoubtedly would have been more productive than meeting again with Harrison, it is little wonder that Tecumseh did not pursue this option. He already had decided to go south and seek new allies among the Creeks and their neighbors, and a trip to Washington would take valuable time. Furthermore, he had no reason to trust that he would receive safe conduct to and from such a meeting. On the contrary, he knew of at least two recent examples of leaders, namely Cornstalk and Moluntha, who gave themselves unarmed into the custody of white authorities, only to be killed. Tecumseh did not intend to allow himself to be that vulnerable. Nevertheless, he did not intend to leave

Prophetstown for the winter without first settling outstanding issues with Harrison. He incorporated Vincennes into his travel route, making it the first stop in his journey south.

Harrison sent a militia officer, Walter Wilson, to find Tecumseh when he did not arrive as expected. Wilson found Tecumseh en route, followed by hundreds of warriors. One portion of the party traveled by water in some fifty-three canoes, while another group came by land. Tecumseh claimed that he had chosen only twenty-four men to escort him and that the rest had decided to come of their own free will; thus, he gave a nod to Harrison's restriction on the number of his group in spirit while ignoring it in fact. It was clear that Tecumseh planned to arrive in Vincennes as an equal to Harrison, well represented and, more to the point, well protected. While on his way to meet Harrison, Tecumseh stopped for a brief visit with the Shakers who lived to the north of the town, who were long-standing friends to him and his people. He at last arrived at the end of July. Tecumseh and his followers, who numbered approximately 320, camped a mile outside Vincennes, while Harrison put the community on full alert and reviewed his militia force, which consisted of nearly 800 men.

The day of the council, Tecumseh and an escort of 180 warriors armed with tomahawks, knives, bows and arrows, and other weapons but no firearms, walked to the arbor that Harrison had constructed as the site of the meeting. To reach the spot, the Native American party walked through streets lined with hundreds of armed militiamen. At the arbor, Harrison waited with 80 dragoons armed with pistols, but without rifles or muskets. For all the show of force and counterforce, the meeting was uneventful. Harrison demanded an explanation for the "confiscation" of the salt annuity that had occurred when the Prophet had taken more than his people's share of the supplies. Tecumseh said that he had not been present in Prophetstown at the time of the salt delivery and that his people had not known what to do. He pointed out that Harrison seemed dissatisfied when his people had refused the annuity the previous year, and now he was dissatisfied that they had accepted it. The discussion ended in a stalemate. Harrison also told Tecumseh that he could solve the current problem of violence and panic by producing the Potawatomis who were guilty of murder. This placed Tecumseh in a difficult situation, since their chief, Main Poc, was also his close ally. He explained to Harrison that the Potawatomis were neither in Prophetstown nor under his authority, but he offered to show his regret for the situation by giving a wampum belt in atonement. He also asked that the whites practice forgiveness, just as he had forgiven the Osages who had killed his relative in order to promote peace. Again, the two were at an impasse.

According to witnesses, Tecumseh spoke well and displayed his characteristic gravity and thoughtfulness during the proceedings. Despite his diplomatic skill, however, he gained nothing from the encounter and gave away more than he realized. His thoughts already were on his trip to the south. He wanted to be certain that nothing important took place in his absence. Before the dialogue concluded, he told Harrison that he had united the northern native nations in a confederacy. Perhaps to alleviate Harrison's concern about this announcement, which was rather premature, he claimed that the United States presented an inspirational model of a union of sovereign peoples, and his people wished to emulate it. He went on to explain that he would be visiting the southern Native Americans that fall and winter in order to unify them in peace, as well. In the interim, he hoped Harrison would not move settlers into the lands purchased via the Fort Wayne Treaty. Many American Indians were in the process of moving to Prophetstown, he noted, and they would need to use this region as hunting grounds. If Harrison would wait, then Tecumseh would return in the spring and help to facilitate all matters. He would speak to President Madison, if necessary. In the meantime, Tecumseh would instruct his people to remain nonviolent and cooperative. He hoped Harrison would do the same.

Tecumseh asked for little more than Harrison had already been instructed to do by his superiors—namely to wait on moving forward with settling the lands on the Wabash and to maintain peace. Harrison, however, heard several new items of information in Tecumseh's speech. First, he learned that additional Native Americans planned to relocate to Prophetstown soon. Even if Tecumseh had exaggerated how many might come, any migration was cause for concern, as it brought more American Indians precisely to the place Harrison wished to be free of them. Larger numbers of followers also meant additional power for Tecumseh and his brother. Second, Harrison learned that Tecumseh would be away for an extended period of time. Even if Tecumseh had exaggerated the degree to which he spoke for all Native Americans, Harrison now appreciated that Tecumseh was the force behind Prophetstown and that without him, the community would be severely weakened.

From these facts, Harrison decided to strike sooner rather than later, while Tecumseh was gone and before more American Indians arrived. Harrison wrote that Tecumseh "is now upon the last round to put a finishing stroke to his work. I hope, however, before his return that that part of the fabric he considered complete will be demolished, and even its foundations rooted up."[2] Before Tecumseh even left Vincennes, Harrison was planning his attack on Prophetstown.

Neither Tecumseh nor the Prophet anticipated Harrison's offensive. Although the Vincennes meeting had brought both sides no closer to compromise, the panic and tension on the frontier seemed to ease. Governor Edwards felt confident enough to release the militia in Illinois territory. No further incidents occurred. Tecumseh went south as he had planned and extolled the strength of Prophetstown to his new audiences, as he shared the message of his confederacy. The Prophet preached to Winnebagos and Kickapoos who had traveled to Prophetstown to hear his teachings. On September 4, 1811, Harrison sent word to the Miamis, Eel Rivers, and Weas at Fort Wayne to withdraw their people from Prophetstown immediately or accept that those who remained could not be protected. He claimed that the earlier murders meant that he had to seek justice and that he would do so by scattering the Prophet's congregation and destroying his anti-U.S. community. He reminded them that the Treaty of Greenville dictated that Native Americans report and resist those who worked against the interest of the United States, and he demanded that they turn their back on the Prophet and his settlement. Harrison's words infuriated his audience, including the Miami leaders Pacanne, Stone Eater, and Big Man and the Wea chiefs Lepousser and Negro Legs, who recognized that Prophetstown sat on unceded land, property that still belonged to the native nations, where Harrison had no right to go. This did not concern Harrison.

The Prophet at last learned of his possible danger and convened a council to ask for advice. He was not in a position of strength. He certainly wished to avoid any problems while Tecumseh was gone; furthermore, despite rumors of stockpiling at the settlement, the Prophet knew that his people possessed only enough ammunition to supply the winter's hunt for food. He was not prepared for a fight. The Prophet and his advisers decided to send a delegation to Vincennes to try to calm Harrison. When the delegation arrived, they learned that a few hotheaded young warriors on the White and Wabash Rivers, possibly Potawatomis, had stolen horses from whites and then engaged the party that pursued them. This gave Harrison an excuse to claim that frontier hostilities were out of control. On September 23 and 24, he met with the Prophetstown delegation. He demanded that the horses be returned and the murderers be surrendered or his army would march on Prophetstown, despite the fact he had no reason to believe that either the animals or the killers were there. The Native American party had little time to attempt negotiation; more than one thousand of Harrison's soldiers were marching immediately on Prophetstown.

At Prophetstown, the Prophet arranged for women, children, and the elderly to move to safety and sent out messengers with orders to call warriors home and seek assistance from neighboring native communities. Scouts and spies reported back to Prophetstown with updates on the movements of the combined force of army regulars and Indiana militia. The troops paused near today's Terre Haute to build Fort Harrison and then continued onward. The Prophet knew his people were outnumbered. Prophetstown boasted only 450 warriors, perhaps less, mostly Shawnees, Winnebagos, and Kickapoos. This number rose somewhat as allied forces from nearby Wyandot, Potawatomi, Piankshaw, and Kickapoo communities arrived to assist their neighbors, but Harrison's men still had the advantage of numbers. The Prophet himself was no warrior, no strategist. He did the one thing he could do: he begged the Great Spirit for help and led his people in spiritual preparations for the coming conflict. While the white soldiers marched, the American Indian warriors conducted ritual purifications and war dances and listened attentively to the exhortations of the Prophet, who promised that the Great Spirit was on their side in the coming conflict.

Harrison expected the Native Americans to be cowed by his large and well-armed offensive force. He did not take into account the psychology of warriors, buoyed by religious ritual and rhetoric, defending their home and faith from what they perceived as invasion. When some Shawnees made their way to Fort Harrison on October 10 and shot one sentry, their determination to protect themselves was clear. So, too, was the anxiety of the white soldiers; a party of Kentucky soldiers chased the Shawnees but returned to Fort Harrison empty-handed, only to be fired upon by their own nervous comrades.

The warriors at Prophetstown might have been preparing psychologically for battle, but the Prophet was not preparing militarily for the conflict. He lacked Tecumseh's talent for strategy. With the exception of one attack on one munitions boat, Harrison's army and their supplies moved unmolested over many miles. Perhaps the Prophet thought that Harrison meant to wait until his latest terms for peace had been answered—these included returning the stolen horses and either surrendering the Potawatomi murderers or proving that they had not been under Prophetstown's protection—but the Prophet also had intelligence that proved the force was on the move. The Prophet did send a message of conciliation in response to the latest message from Harrison, but the party dispatched with it missed its intended audience. Even the evacuation of the village was incomplete. The American Indians had accomplished one thing, however: building a breastwork around the settlement, with log fortifications shielding trenches for gunmen.

Upon reaching Prophetstown, Harrison called for a talk. The Prophet sent three other leaders to speak with him and to reiterate that the people of Prophetstown had no desire for violence. Harrison agreed to a more formal conference the following day and camped at present-day Battleground, approximately one mile northwest of the village. His troops and their equipment covered nearly ten acres of the high ground along Burnett's Creek. They did not erect breastworks around the camp but arranged themselves in a defensive position and slept clothed, with weapons at the ready.

Despite the fact Harrison had agreed to discuss peace the following day, the Native Americans in Prophetstown were wary. They completed the evacuation of noncombatants that night and debated their options. Apparently a key figure in determining the Prophetstown strategy was a black cook named Ben, a man who had served with Harrison's forces. Historians remain uncertain whether Ben was a deserter or a captured prisoner; either way, he told the Prophet and his advisers a great deal about Harrison's forces and camp. It seems likely that Ben also claimed that Harrison intended not to meet the following morning, but rather to launch a surprise attack on Prophetstown.

It is clear that the Prophet feared that Harrison would move against the community the next day. Badly outmanned and outgunned, his people had only the advantage of surprise. According to contemporary accounts, he told his warriors that the Great Spirit sanctioned a night attack. Although they faced a foe of double their numbers, the Native Americans had the advantage, because the Great Spirit would make them impervious to bullets and would make certain that they could see while their enemy remained blinded. No doubt some recalled Blue Jacket's impressive victory against might odds in 1791 and dreamed of similar glory. It is probable, though not certain, that the Kickpaoo Mengoatowa and the Winnebago Waweapakoosa volunteered to lead the strike. And so, on the night of November 6 and the morning of November 7, 1811, a multitribal force of Shawnees, Kickapoos, Winnebagos, Potawatomis, Piankeshaws, Wyandots, Iroquois, Ottawas, and Ojibwes—as many as 500 warriors—moved into position around Harrison's camp, with faces blackened to blend into the night.

At approximately 4:30 in the morning, a U.S. sentry glimpsed something in the woods and fired. The American Indians charged into the camp. Harrison himself helped to reinforce the northwest corner of the camp. Fighting was frenzied in the predawn gloom, made murkier by the smoke of firearms. For a time the American Indians had the advantage, as they dispersed U.S. horses and cattle and picked off soldiers who were illuminated by the camp fires. The troops, however, formed able lines of defense quickly, especially the portion of the force made up of U.S. army regulars. They were able to slow the advance of the Prophetstown warriors long enough for the sun to rise, giving Harrison's men a view of their opponents and their numbers, or lack thereof. Harrison's army then launched a counterattack. After over two hours of desperate fighting, the American Indians had little remaining ammunition. They gathered their wounded and dead and retreated toward Prophetstown, thus ending the Battle of Tippecanoe. They had made a spirited defense of the community; Harrison had 188 casualties, far more than the American Indians' estimated 50. Without ammunition or the benefit of surprise, however, there was no further hope of defending Prophetstown.

When Harrison's army reached Prophetstown, on November 8, they found its inhabitants gone. All evidence pointed to a hasty but thorough flight. Harrison ordered his men to seize equipment such as cooking implements and to use what corn they needed. They burned the homes, buildings, and granaries. The refugees from Prophetstown would have no shelter, no food stores, and no ammunition for hunting. On November 9, Harrison ordered his soldiers home to Vincennes, leaving the heart of Tecumseh's confederacy in ashes.

NOTES

1. Quoted in John Sudgen, *Tecumseh: A Life* (New York: Henry Holt, 1997), p. 215.

2. Ibid., p. 225.

Chapter 7

THE STORM OF WAR

When Tecumseh left the conference with Harrison at Vincennes, he began a tour of historic proportions on behalf of his cause. With him came six Shawnees, six Winnebagos, six Kickapoos, and two Creek guides. Over a six-month period, he visited lands that would become at least 10 U.S. states, perhaps more, meeting with different communities and councils. In this three-thousand-mile odyssey—undertaken when travel meant the uncertainty and vulnerability of open country, riding for hours, camping in the wilderness, and living off the land—Tecumseh proved why he is remembered above all others as a champion of pan-tribal unity. Leaders planned and organized confederacies before Tecumseh, but no one approached the challenge on such a scale or with such unflagging energy, dedication, and vision.

From Vincennes, Tecumseh journeyed into what is today northern Alabama. There he met with several leaders, including the mixed-blood George Colbert. Colbert and his comrades showed great respect to Tecumseh and listened to his presentations with attention, but ultimately they would not join Tecumseh's confederacy. Several factors influenced their reaction to Tecumseh's message. First, the Chickasaws considered both the Kickapoos and the Shawnees to be historical enemies; it was a testament to Tecumseh's stature, in fact, that they had welcomed him with such hospitality. Joining the confederacy, however, meant partnering with native nations that the Chickasaws traditionally considered as hostile as the United States, if not more so. Furthermore, the Chickasaws—one of the so-called Five Civilized Tribes, along with the Choctaws, the Creeks, the Cherokees, and the Seminoles—had moved far along the path of assimilating Anglo culture. Although they had a strong desire to protect their property, they had little interest in the conservative nativism of Tecumseh's movement, especially as it was manifested in the teachings of the Prophet. With Colbert's guidance, the Chickasaws declined Tecumseh's invitation to join him, but they were impressed enough to honor him with an escort, which assisted him in reaching other villages and continuing his recruitment tour.

The Choctaws, who lived in present-day Mississippi, were not as gracious as the Chickasaws. Of the southern native nations, the Choctaws were the greatest supporters of the United States and thus the most hostile to Tecumseh's message. Their negative feelings toward Great Britain were such that they had even helped the colonists and their French and Spanish allies during the War of Independence. Since that time, the Choctaws had developed close ties to their local U.S. Indian agents and to Christian missionaries. Many had adopted the so-called yeoman farmer lifestyle and become living embodiments of the U.S. civilization campaign. Among the Chickasaws, Colbert disagreed with Tecumseh quietly and firmly, with courtesy and goodwill. When Tecumseh spoke among the Choctaws, however, he found the powerful war chief Pushmataha offering a loud rebuttal to his every speech. When Tecumseh traveled to another village, Pushmataha followed so that he could challenge Tecumseh's presentation at his next destination. In formal councils at Mokalusha, Chunky's Town, and Moshulitubbee's Town, Pushmataha, who possessed close connections with U.S. officials, stirred his listeners with militant rhetoric against the British and against the northern native nations. As Tecumseh's tour progressed, the mixed-blood leaders David Folsum and John Pitchlyn joined forces with Pushmataha. At last, Tecumseh moved on from the Choctaw villages, with few followers to show for his efforts.

Next Tecumseh began a trek through the Creek nation, a trip destined to be more influential than Tecumseh could have imagined. The Creeks spread out from central Georgia through what is now Alabama. They were organized in a loose union of culturally connected villages of Muskogees, Alabamas, Hitchitis, and Yuchis, among others. The Creek nation was divided into two distinct regional groups, each of which developed into a political faction. The Lower Creeks located their homes along the Chattahoochee and Flint Rivers. They had adopted many British and U.S. customs, and they looked particularly to the U.S. Indian agent Benjamin Hawkins for leadership. The Upper Creeks, who lived along the Tallapoosa and Coosa Rivers, lived in a more traditional fashion and were less acculturated to the white lifestyle. Most of them strongly resented the recent building of a U.S. federal road—a project supported by Benjamin Hawkins and the Lower Creeks—that cut through their property to connect the state of Georgia to the cities of Mobile and New Orleans. Although the Upper Creek Chief Big Warrior received a steady income from tolls and thus did not fight the road, most of the warriors opposed it because it encouraged white traffic and settlement near, and sometimes on, Creek lands.

Tecumseh already shared a unique affinity with the Upper Creeks, because many Shawnees, including his parents, had lived among them in the period after the Shawnees had scattered from the Ohio Valley, fleeing war. At the central village of Tuckabatchee, he met an enthusiastic welcome, including a number of warriors who were ready to join him on the spot. He did not count on quick or easy success, however. In 1793, Chief Red Pole had led a delegation to these same Creeks to invite them to participate in the pan-tribal alliance organized in the north, and the Creeks had not only declined the offer but also fought the party. Tecumseh was aware that Big Warrior was not altogether pleased with his appearance, as it threatened his lucrative tolls; it seems that Tecumseh also realized that Benjamin Hawkins had assigned the Creek mixed-blood William McIntosh to spy on him and his talk. Tecumseh prepared to speak to a large, formal council session at Tuckabatchee but postponed his presentation until McIntosh at last left the village in frustration. Then, to an assembled crowd of several thousand, Tecumseh made his plea for Native unity.

Although the exact text of his speech is lost, the substance remains in several different accounts of the historic night. Tecumseh immediately began by drawing parallels between his people and the Creeks. He offered a detailed list of injustices suffered by the Creeks as well as the northern native nations, perpetrated by the U.S. government and by white settlers. The main grievances he underscored were the taking of Native American land, the killing of American Indian game, and the threatening of traditional native culture. All the means by which Native America could survive—politically, economically, socially—were under attack, he explained. He asked his audience members to join him in his confederacy, to cooperate with the other native nations in common action, and to return to the lifestyles and beliefs of their ancestors. He assured them that when war broke out between the United States and Great Britain—and this was a question of when, not if—Great Britain would help them fight the United States. The results of such a conflict, he said, would be the restoration of lost lands, prosperity, and dignity. Tecumseh invited one of his guides, who also served as an interpreter, to address the assembly after him. It is likely that this man was born a Creek, even if he had lived for years among other peoples. The interpreter was especially inspired by the teachings of the Prophet and put the religious revitalization message of Prophetstown into context with the larger pan-tribal movement Tecumseh championed.

The Creeks reacted very favorably to what they heard. Their experiences had made them very receptive to the ideas that political and military unity were necessary for the protection of Native American lands and that shunning white influences and returning to traditional practices would help to restore their people to their previous power and prestige. The added apocalyptic vision of the Prophet, that supernatural powers would push back the United States and restore the continent to the native nations, added hope, as did the far more earthly promise of British arms and ammunition. Yet another influence helped Tecumseh's reception among the Creeks. Throughout September 1811, while Tecumseh visited Creek villages, a comet appeared in the sky. This is a scientific fact; the massive comet was seen and verified all over the world. To those in the U.S. south, it grew brighter throughout November, as Tecumseh addressed Creek councils. Of course, many made the connection that "Tecumtha" meant "Shooting Star"; Tecumseh himself claimed that the heavenly vision was an omen that foreshadowed bad fortune for his enemies. Immediately after Tecumseh left the Creeks, the comet faded from view, as if to confirm that the skies recognized and responded to his power and promise.

At his final presentation to the Creeks, Tecumseh asked the warriors to prepare for battle and then await word from him. All would be lost if the fighting broke out too soon. He said he would send a message when the time was right, and all of the nations would rise up and strike together as one confederacy. He left them with this vision of unified Native American resistance. A number of Creek warriors followed him as members of his party. His guide and interpreter remained with the Creeks as a kind of ambassador.

Certainly Tecumseh did not foresee the significant and long-lasting effects his visit would have on the Creek nation. The mixed-blood Creeks of partial Scotch-Irish background, for example, felt a strong connection to Tecumseh's message. Many had reason to resent U.S. treatment of their families doubly. As Native Americans and Loyalist British sympathizers, neither side of their ancestry was especially welcomed in mainstream U.S. society. One of these Scotch-Irish Creeks, Josiah Francis, claimed to have a vision similar to the Prophet's shortly after Tecumseh's visit. He began spreading his nativist teachings among the Creeks, and a new religious revitalization movement began. Followers of Francis became Red Sticks, so named because of the red-stained war clubs they carried. They formed a militant faction that resisted and sabotaged the U.S. civilization program in any way possible. Tecumseh had unwittingly provided the Red Sticks with a catalogue of injuries suffered at the hands of the United States, a strategy for striking back, and a spiritual justification for resistance.

Tecumseh's appearance and inspiration widened the breach between the Upper and Lower Creeks. When some of the Creek warriors who left to follow Tecumseh returned to their people the following year, they took a detour and killed several white settlers near Nashville. Other Creeks, including Big Warrior himself, fought against them. The conflict between the nativists and the assimilationists, the Red Sticks and the White Sticks, evolved into full-scale civil war among the Creeks. The Red Stick War pitted Creeks against other Creeks and the United States. The conflict did not end until March 1814, when Andrew Jackson led a combination of U.S. soldiers and pro-U.S. American Indian warriors to victory at the bloody Battle of Horseshoe Bend and then promptly used the war as a justification for taking Creek lands. Tecumseh did not survive to see this unintended outcome of his influence, but it is certain that he would have grieved over it. He was not a warmonger by nature, although he could motivate men to arms with great gusto when needed; in fact, he turned to war only when he despaired of any positive result from diplomacy. What he feared and hated most, however, was the thought of American Indians fighting American Indians.

Historians remain uncertain about how Tecumseh spent the next two months. According to some oral accounts, he traveled in the Cherokee nation, perhaps as far east as North Carolina, but these reports are not specific and in places contradict verifiable information. He no doubt was sharing the word about his confederacy, wherever he roamed. He appeared next in the Missouri area, revisiting the Shawnee and Delaware villages there. While he was in Missouri, a series of shocks rocked the earth from Canada to the Gulf of Mexico. Known as the New Madrid Earthquakes, these shocks produced bizarre effects that seemed completely unnatural to those who saw them: fissures opening in the ground and shooting forth sand and water; animals congregating alongside the species that preyed upon them; birds landing on humans' heads and shoulders and refusing to fly. These uncanny events appeared to suggest the supernatural.

To the Creeks in the south, the quakes seemed to punctuate Tecumseh's pleas for his fellow Natives to change their lifestyles and his exhortations for them to resist the powers that deprived them of their lands and self-respect. Tecumseh had left them only weeks before the disastrous shocks were felt, and his blend of practical politics and supernatural vision gave them a means to understand the violent natural events that they witnessed. Soon, some Creeks claimed that Tecumseh had predicted the earthquakes, or promised Big Warrior that he would stomp his foot so that the Creek leader felt it all the way in Tuckabatchee, or claimed that he would climb a mountain and shake the earth as a message to those who followed him. Much like the comet, the earthquakes became a part of Creek legend, magnifying the importance of Tecumseh. The skies above and the ground below recognized him as a chosen leader, it seemed.

Tecumseh was near the epicenter of the quakes in Missouri. The local native nations interpreted the shocks in terms of the Prophet's end of the world scenario. Perhaps the earthquakes were a sign that the world would come to an end soon and that supernatural powers would wipe away the whites and the unworthy American Indians, leaving only the righteous Native Americans to regain their lands and past prosperity. It followed, then, that the best course of action was to renounce white ways, revive traditional customs, and ally with other groups who were doing the same. Surely these ideas made the nearby villagers unusually open to Tecumseh's message.

After retreading familiar paths among the Shawnees and the Delawares, Tecumseh undertook a mission to the Osages. This trip was particularly dangerous for several reasons. First, violent conflict between the Osages and the Missouri Shawnees remained ongoing. Not only was Tecumseh Shawnee himself, but also he had just come from meeting with the Missouri Shawnees—with the enemy, as the Osages would see it. Second, some Osages previously had killed one of Tecumseh's relatives. In the interest of promoting unity, Tecumseh relinquished his personal right to blood vengeance, but he did not know how this would be perceived by the Osages. Perhaps they did not believe this renunciation was true, or perhaps they viewed it less as a heroic choice for peace than as a cowardly choice for self-preservation.

Tecumseh was welcomed and allowed to speak in council, however. John D. Hunter, who was a white captive of the Osages at the time, later regained his freedom and wrote a book, *Memoirs of a Captivity among the Indians of North America*. This volume included an eyewitness description of Tecumseh's address, one that might well have applied to many of the speeches Tecumseh gave as he toured the villages and councils of Native America. For such a presentation, Tecumseh tapped into his warrior persona; if war was necessary, he would not be halfhearted in its pursuit. Although this account is not a precise transcript, Hunter's summary provides a useful window into Tecumseh's message and its reception:

> He [Tecumseh] addressed them in long, eloquent, and pathetic strains; and an assembly more numerous than had ever been witnessed on any former occasion listened to him with an intensely agitated, though profoundly respectful interest and attention. In fact, so great was the effect produced by Tecum-seh's eloquence, that the chiefs adjourned the council, shortly after he had closed his harangue; nor did they finally come to a decision on the great question in debate for days afterwards.
>
> I wish it was in my power to do justice to the eloquence of this distinguished man: but it is utterly impossible. The richest colours, shaded with a master's pencil, would fall infinitely short of the glowing finish of the original. The occasion and subject were particularly adapted to call into action all the powers of genuine patriotism; and such language, such gestures, and such feelings and fullness of soul contending for utterance, were exhibited by this untutored native of the forest in the central wilds of America, as no audience, I am persuaded, either in ancient or modern times ever before witnessed.
>
> My readers may think some qualification due to this opinion; but none is necessary. The unlettered Te-cum-seh gave extemporaneous utterance only to what he felt; it was a simple, but vehement narration of the wrongs imposed by the white people on the Indians, and an exhortation for the latter to resist them. The whole addressed to an audience composed of individuals who had been educated to prefer almost any sacrifice to that of personal liberty, and even death to the degradation of their nation; and who, in this occasion, felt the portraiture of Te-cum-seh but too strikingly identified with their own conditions, wrongs, and sufferings.
>
> This discourse made an impression on my mind which, I think, will last as long as I live. I cannot repeat it *verbatim*, though if I could, it would be a mere skeleton, without the rounding finish of its integuments; it would only be the shadow of the substance; because the gestures, and the interest and feelings excited by the occasion, and which constitute the essentials of its character, would be altogether wanting. Nevertheless, I shall, as far as my recollection serves, make the attempt,

and trust to the indulgence of my readers for an apology for the presumptuous digression.

SPEECH TO THE OSAGES

When the Osages and distinguished strangers had assembled, Te-cum-she arose; and after a pause of some minutes, in which he surveyed his audience in a very dignified, though respectfully complaisant and sympathizing manner, he commenced as follows:

"*Brothers*,—We all belong to one family; we are all children of the Great Spirit; we walk in the same path; slake our thirst at the same spring; and now affairs of the greatest concern lead us to smoke the pipe around the same council fire!

"*Brothers*,—We are friends; we must assist each other to bear our burdens. The blood of many of our fathers and brothers has run like water on the ground, to satisfy the avarice of the white men. We, ourselves, are threatened with a great evil; nothing will pacify them but the destruction of all the red men.

"*Brothers*,—When the white men first set foot on our grounds, they were hungry; they had no place on which to spread their blankets, or to kindle their fires. They were feeble; they could do nothing for themselves. Our father commiserated their distress, and shared freely with them whatever the Great Spirit had given his red children. They gave them food when hungry, medicine when sick, spread skins for them to sleep on, and gave them grounds, that they might hunt and raise corn.

"*Brothers*,—Brothers the white people came among us feeble, and now we have made them strong, they wish to kill us, or drive us back, as they would wolves and panthers.

"*Brothers*,—The white men are not friends to the Indians: at first, they only asked for land sufficient for a wigwam; now, nothing will satisfy them but the whole of our hunting grounds, from the rising to the setting sun.

"*Brothers*,—The white men want more than our hunting grounds; they wish to kill our warriors; they would even kill our old men, women and little ones.

"*Brothers*,—Many winters ago, there was no land; the sun did not rise and set: all was darkness. The Great Spirit made all things. He gave the white people a home beyond the great waters. He supplied these grounds with game, and gave them to his red children; and he gave them strength and courage to defend them.

"*Brothers*,—My people wish for peace; the red men all wish for peace; but where the white people are, there is no peace for them, except it be the bosom of our mother.

"*Brothers*,—The white men despise and cheat the Indians; they abuse and insult them; they do not think the red men sufficiently good to live.

"*Brothers*,—The red men have borne many and great injuries; they ought to suffer them no longer. My people will not; they are determined on vengeance; they will drink the blood of the white people.

"*Brothers*,—My people are brave and numerous; but the white people are too strong for them alone. I wish you to take up the tomahawk with them. If we all unite, we will cause the rivers to stain the great waters with their blood.

"*Brothers*,—if you do not unite with us, they will first destroy us, and then you will an easy prey to them. They have destroyed many nations of red men because they were not united, because they were not friends to each other.

"*Brothers*,—The white people send runners amongst us; they wish to make us enemies that they may sweep over and desolate our hunting grounds, like devastating winds, or rushing waters.

"*Brothers*,—Our Great Father, over the great waters, is angry with the white people, our enemies. He will send his brave warriors against them; he will send us rifles, and whatever else we want—he is our friend, and we are his children.

"*Brothers*,—Who are the white people that we should fear them? They cannot run fast, and are good marks to shoot at: they are only men; our fathers have killed many of them; we are not squaws, and we will stain the earth red with blood.

"*Brothers*,—The Great Spirit is angry with our enemies; he speaks in thunder, and the earth swallows up villages, and drinks up the Mississippi. The great waters will cover their lowlands; their corn cannot grow; and the Great Spirit will sweep those who escape to the hills from the earth with his terrible breath.

"*Brothers*,—We must be united; we must smoke the same pipe; we must fight each other' battles; and more than all, we must love the Great Spirit; he is for us; he will destroy our enemies, and make all his red children happy."[1]

The Osages gave serious consideration to Tecumseh's invitation, which was in itself a victory. They decided at last that they would not join the confederacy, but the council was not altogether a loss, as it forged a new line of communication between Tecumseh and the Osages. It also proved that there was interest in and sympathy for Tecumseh's cause, even if the Osages felt the time was not right for them to act.

At some point during this time, Tecumseh learned the news about the Battle of Tippecanoe and the burning of Prophetstown. Historians do not know the details of how he received the information. It seems he originally planned to return to Prophetstown after visiting the Osages, but he changed his mind upon hearing that he had no home, in effect, to which he could return. True to form, Tecumseh threw himself into another round of visitations, as if to begin rebuilding what was destroyed and to revive the morale of his followers. His new message, added to the old, was that reports of the death of his confederacy were premature. He retraced his past journeys and stopped at villages where he had significant support. In a short period he had touched base with the Iowas, the Kickapoos, the Potawatomis, the Ojibwes, the Ottawas, the Sacs, and the Santee Dakota Sioux. His message to the warriors in each settlement was twofold: those who wished to follow him immediately were welcome to come, but those who did not needed to refrain from pointless violence and maintain the peace until the time came for collective, orchestrated action. U.S. officials remained nervous, aware that he was traveling quickly over great distances, moving among his people, and meeting success with his recruitment efforts.

Tecumseh did not return to the Wabash until late January of 1812. Only then did he see firsthand the ruins of Prophetstown and learn the true extent of the losses there. The warriors had used nearly all of their ammunition. The U.S. soldiers had destroyed the homes, the community buildings, and the food stores and had taken many tools and implements. Perhaps worst of all, the U.S. forces had dug up American Indian graves, leaving the dead bodies of the slain to rot above the ground, desecrating the burial site and dishonoring the fallen warriors. Tecumseh was shaken. According to one credible account, often recounted by biographers, Tecumseh seized his younger brother by the hair and threatened to kill him for what he had allowed to happen. In fact, Tecumseh did not need to worry about what to do with the Prophet; he was his own worst enemy. Although the Creeks hundreds of miles removed from Prophetstown now built upon the foundation of his spiritual teachings, the Prophet had become almost irrelevant in his own homeland.

Those warriors who had fought in the Battle of Tippecanoe recalled how the Prophet had promised them that the Great Spirit would lead them to miraculous victory. They discovered through painful experience that they were neither invisible to U.S. eyes nor impervious to U.S. bullets. Furthermore, the Prophet had remained behind in the settlement, interceding on their behalf with the Great Spirit, rather than risking life and limb with his people. Perhaps, some said, he was not a holy man at all but merely a coward. Those who survived and felt betrayed by the Prophet confronted him. He responded by blaming one of his wives; he claimed that she had, without his knowledge, contaminated his sacred ceremony, because she was menstruating (and thus unclean). This weak defense was scorned as such. The warriors let him live, but after Tippecanoe he was, for the most part, a man of little consequence in the eyes of the community—which was, for a man of his personality and character, a bitter thing to accept.

For those who had once lived in Prophetstown, the winter was remarkably difficult. Almost immediately, the survivors split into small parties and devoted themselves to the hunt, recognizing how challenging it would be to obtain sufficient food for the winter. The weather added to their misery with unusual cold and heavy snowfall. In the Indiana region, those Native Americans who were not active supporters of Tecumseh's movement appealed to Fort Wayne for annuities and assistance. Some groups, such as the Weas and the Miamis, interceded on behalf of those who were ardent followers of Tecumseh in order to secure supplies and help for them, as well. From Vincennes, Harrison announced that if the American Indians expelled both the Prophet and Tecumseh from their communities and went home—in other words, not back to Prophetstown—peace would be preserved. Tecumseh agreed to this and urged the local Kickapoos, Piankeshaws, Winnebagos, and others to go along with Harrison's demands. He seemed glad that he could help buy time for his followers to recuperate from their losses, even if it was only by maintaining a low profile, and he encouraged them to appease Harrison in the short term in order to survive.

As Tecumseh worried about how his people would survive the winter, Harrison declared to his superiors and the press that at the Battle of Tippecanoe he had won a decisive victory. He claimed that this success meant the end of American Indian attacks on white settlements, a final solution to the problem of frontier violence. Not everyone agreed with him. For example, John Randolph of Roanoke blamed the United States for the so-called Indian war, and Congressman Thomas Worthington of Ohio, who had met and negotiated with Tecumseh in 1807, referred to Tippecanoe as a sad event. In January 1812, Harrison received new orders from Secretary of War William Eustis. He was to pursue peace talks, saying that the president was angry about the recent bloodshed and prepared to send more troops if necessary but that he desired only peace. If the Native Americans agreed not to fight the United States in the future, they should be pardoned for all past actions. Madison clearly wanted Harrison to do everything possible to secure a stable and lasting peace. The president also invited Tecumseh, the Prophet, and additional American Indian chiefs to Washington, D.C., in order to discuss the situation in person.

When Tecumseh learned of this invitation to the U.S. capital—made with the specific condition that he could not be the leader of the Native American party—he demurred, telling Harrison that he would like to go but that he needed to wait until later in the spring, after he had helped plant the new corn crop. In truth, Tecumseh never planned to visit Washington, D.C. This was unfortunate, since such a trip would have allowed him to circumvent the local and regional officials and their self-interested agendas and speak directly to a national leader who was well aware of his need for Native American allies in the forthcoming conflict with Great Britain. For a time, Madison appeared genuinely to be interested in appeasing and compromising with Native America. Tecumseh did not desire war, but he had lost all faith in negotiation at any level. His veiled rejection of the invitation arguably was born more of despair than of hostility. The American Indian party never made it to Washington, with or without Tecumseh.

It soon became to clear to everyone who kept abreast of national events that Harrison was wrong when he asserted that the Battle of Tippecanoe had ended violent conflict on the frontier. On the contrary, aside from the physical destruction of Prophetstown, Tippecanoe was a complete failure for the United States. After all, Harrison had not gained custody of the murderers he sought. He had not cowed the Native Americans with his display of force; they had attacked first and fought bravely, and the army's desecration of the American Indian graves suggested cowardice, not prowess, to the native nations. By digging up the dead, destroying the food supplies, and stealing tools and implements, Harrison's force exacerbated American Indian anger and desperation. In short, Tippecanoe led to more, not less, bloodshed on the frontier.

Beginning in early spring, various raids occurred all over the region. Harrison had claimed that the violent incidents before Tippecanoe were out of control; this was one reason he used to justify marching on Prophetstown. In 1810 and 1811, before the battle, only eight or nine whites were killed by American Indians in the area. But in the six months after the confrontation, a total of forty-six whites were killed by Native Americans in the territories of Louisiana, Illinois, Indiana, and Ohio. Although these murders were geographically diverse, a common thread linked them; all of the killings were conducted by individuals who belonged to native nations represented in the Battle of Tippecanoe. Tecumseh was not behind these killings. He found them both embarrassing to his cause and impossible to stop. They were fueled by pure fury, nothing short of revenge killings for deaths at and desecrated graves after the Battle of Tippecanoe.

In May 1812, Tecumseh took part in an intertribal conference on the Mississinewa River near the Wabash about this epidemic of bloodshed. Representatives of many nations—Delawares, Eel Rivers, Kickapoos, Ojibwes, Ottawas, Piankeshaws, Potawatomis, Shawnees, Miamis, Weas, Winnebagos, and Wyandots (or Hurons)—attended. Isidore Chaine, a mixed-blood Wyandot, came from the north specifically to represent the British position. Chaine reminded the attendees that the British disapproved of hostile actions toward the United States. In fact, the British knew that war would break out between their country and the United States very shortly, but they did not wish for the mercurial Native American situation to rush or complicate the conflict. Chaine conveyed the message that the British were very sorry for the losses and challenges the American Indians had experienced. Great Britain did not and would not, however, support the idea of Native Americans going to war against the United States.

Tecumseh seized the opportunity to show publicly his outrage at recent events. In so doing, he appeared to be genuinely on the side of peace. In reality, Tecumseh did not seek or thrive on conflict; he simply wanted his people to be left alone on their lands to pursue their lives. By 1812, however, he was convinced by all he had seen, heard, and experienced that war was the only answer to U.S. expansionism. Nonetheless, he took the chance this conference afforded to speak against cowardly, thoughtless bloodshed. He said several things of note. First, he placed the blame for the original violence on the Potawatomis. According to the official U.S. Indian Department transcription of the English translation of his speech, Tecumseh said, "We have not brought these misfortunes on ourselves; We have done nothing wrong, but we will now point out to You those who have occasioned all the mischief. Our Younger Brothers the Potawatomis (pointing to them) in spite of our repeated counsel to them to remain quiet and live in peace with the Big Knives, would not listen to us."[2]

Furthermore, he was openly critical of his brother, the Prophet, and the way in which he had handled (or mishandled) the confrontation with Harrison:

> When I left home last Year to go to the Creek Nation, I passed at Post Vincennes and was stopped by the Big Knives, and did not immediately know the reason, but I was soon informed that the Potawatomis had killed some of their people. I told the Big Knives to remain quiet until my return, when I should make peace and quietness prevail. On my return I found my Village reduced to ashes by the Big Knives. You cannot blame Your Younger Brothers the Shawanee [sic] for what has happened, the Potawatomis occasioned the misfortune. Had I been at home and heard of the advance of the American Troops to-wards our Village, I should have gone to meet them and shaking them by the hand, have asked them the reason of their appearance in such hostile guise.
>
> Father & Brothers! You tell us to retreat or turn to one side should the Big Knives come against us. Had I been at home in the late unfortunate affair I should have done, but those I left at home were (I cannot call them men) a poor set of people, and their scuffle with the Big Knives I compare to a struggle between little children who only scratch each others [sic] faces.[3]

Some who attended the conference denounced Tecumseh, or at least distanced themselves from his cause. This was not entirely unexpected: among them were chiefs who had lost warriors, and thus power over their communities, thanks to Tecumseh. Many more criticized the Prophet. When this happened, however, the Native Americans seemed to draw a clear distinction between Tecumseh and his brother. The Prophet's shame did not transfer automatically either to Tecumseh or his pan-tribal resistance movement. Moreover, some of the attacks leveled at Tecumseh were for political purposes only; it was wise to speak against him in certain public spheres, to deflect attention from what Tecumseh was doing and planning to do, and to minimize the degree to which he was perceived by non-Natives as a threat. Criticism of the Prophet, on the other hand, apparently was bitter and heartfelt.

Although Tecumseh spoke for peace during the meeting, his final words conveyed a more ominous, arguably honest tone: "If we hear of the Big Knives coming towards our villages to speak peace, we will receive them, but if We hear of any of our people being hurt by them, or if they unprovokedly advance against us in a hostile manner, be assured we will defend ourselves like men. And if we hear of any of our people having been killed, We will immediately send to all the Nations on or towards the Mississippi, and all this Island will rise as one man. Then Father and Brothers it will be impossible for You or either of You to restore peace between us."[4] Before the gathering dispersed, Chaine pulled Tecumseh aside with words from the British meant especially for his ears. Chaine confirmed that war between Great Britain and the United States was inevitable. Until it occurred, however, the British wanted Tecumseh to do all he could to keep his people calm and peaceable. Tecumseh replied that he planned shortly to journey to Canada himself and to speak to Matthew Elliott at Fort Malden.

After that, things happened quickly. On June 1, 1812, U.S. President James Madison shared with Congress a list of grievances the United States had against Great Britain. All were related to maritime issues save one: the United States blamed Great Britain for working with Tecumseh to agitate and inflame Native Americans and to promote hostility on the frontier. Tecumseh made one last and quite successful sweep of the nearby native nations, during which he gained an estimated 350 additional warriors from the Potawatomis and the Miamis alone. It was clear that Tecumseh intended to launch a war with the United States, with or without the backing of the British in Canada. Before leaving to go north, Tecumseh organized delegations of warriors, chosen to represent all of the native nations in his confederacy, to journey forth to other Native Americans and meet with various councils and villages. These ambassadors of Tecumseh's carried black wampum belts and red-painted tobacco to share with their audiences as invitations to war. Those with whom they met in turn sent out other messengers to reach yet more native nations. Tecumseh's parties reached as far as what would become Nebraska on their errand of diplomacy.

Because of the secrecy and speed with which the messages passed during this time, it is difficult to recreate Tecumseh's master plan with any certainty. Various interviews and accounts suggest that contacts across the land received word of plans for simultaneous attacks by Native American armies in the United States. Historians' current best guess is that at least four separate major offensives were expected: one in Louisiana territory, one in Michigan territory, one in Illinois territory (probably led by Main Poc), and one in Indiana territory (probably led by Tecumseh personally). These attacks together would have involved thousands of American Indian warriors representing a variety of native nations.

It is difficult to determine if the secretive talk and furtive rumors of this time exaggerated the scale of Tecumseh's support. In a way, it may have served as a self-fulfilling prophecy; by sharing the expectation of large numbers of warriors coordinating simultaneous strikes, confederacy members may have drawn more warriors into the movement to take part in these campaigns. It is certain that groups of warriors devoted to Tecumseh began to concentrate in various key locations, including the ruins of Prophetstown. Some of these places boasted far more than a thousand warriors. Current estimates indicate that this network represented a larger confederacy than the pan-tribal union in 1763–1764, and, though it may have been comparable in numbers to the intertribal efforts of the 1780s and 1790s, it was far more inclusive, involving western nations such as the Winnebagos and the Dakotas, which had not previously been engaged with such movements. From the north to the south, from the borders of the frontier west, the Tecumseh confederacy anticipated one united war with the United States.

En route to Amherstburg, Tecumseh paused at Fort Wayne to speak with the new Indian agent there, Benjamin Stickney, most likely to banish any fears the man might have had about his absence and to be certain that those who were congregating in the remains of Prophetstown would be safe while he was gone. Tecumseh readily admitted that he was traveling north, but he claimed that his major purpose for the trip was to promote peace among the Wyandots, the Ottawas, and the Ojibwes in Michigan territory. While at Fort Wayne, Tecumseh learned that the territorial governor of Michigan, William Hull, was leading a large army north from Urbana in Ohio in order to reinforce the defenses of Detroit. The fact that this large force was on the march made Tecumseh's journey all the more dangerous but also all the more necessary. With war between the United States and Great Britain on its way, it seemed the best time possible for Tecumseh to pursue his goal of forging a pan-tribal Native American alliance with Great Britain against the United States.

On June 18, 1812, before Tecumseh left Fort Wayne, the United States formally declared war. This made even visiting Fort Malden a hostile act in the eyes of the United States. Tecumseh went anyway.

On July 1, Tecumseh reached Amherstburg. He was not far ahead of the U.S. army; five days later, Hull reached Detroit. Tecumseh found Main Poc and other chiefs waiting for him with their warriors. Their commitment contrasted sharply with the indecision of the Wyandots at Brownstown, however. These Wyandots occupied a crucial position, as Brownstown sat below the U.S. forces at Detroit and directly across from the British forces at Fort Malden. If the Wyandots did not support Tecumseh's confederacy and the British, then the leadership had a perfect opportunity to spy on the allies and report their movements to U.S. forces. Tecumseh, who enjoyed great success in wooing the Wyandot warriors but suffered outright censure from some of the Wyandot chiefs, threw his energies into recruiting all of the Wyandots to his side. At last, he convinced Chief Walk-in-the-Water to join the confederacy, and he went to Fort Malden with his warriors to support Tecumseh and the British. This was a real victory in terms of strategy, but it was also a symbolic victory, because Brownstown, the seat of the Northwest Confederacy, had joined the fight. Walk-in-the-Water proved to be an untrustworthy ally, however.

Some things had changed in Canada since Tecumseh had last visited. Sir George Prevost had replaced Sir James Craig as governor-general, for example, and Brigadier-General Isaac Brock had taken command of all forces in Upper Canada. Now in his seventies, the old Scot Matthew Elliott—a neighbor to, trader with, and husband of Shawnees, as well as a speaker of the Shawnee tongue—was still there. He recognized Tecumseh as the chief of chiefs, and he became a permanent fixture at Tecumseh's side through the Battle of the Thames. From Amherstburg, the British and the American Indians learned that Hull planned to invade Canada from Detroit. Hull believed he could take British provisions for his men while gaining control of key positions in Canada. He expected that Canadians would rally to the U.S. flag—were they not, after all, colonials who should be liberated from their oppressive motherland?—and that a few early victories might intimidate the American Indians and cause them to rethink their alliance with Great Britain. Brock, who was also serving as lieutenant governor, learned to his distress that the provincial legislature, without a shot being fired, assumed Canada would fall. It planned no resistance so as not to antagonize the United States.

For a man who had worked tirelessly for unity among his people, it must have been remarkably poignant for Tecumseh to meet with the Shawnee James Logan on July 7. Tecumseh knew and liked Logan personally. Logan was north with a small party of the Wapakoneta Shawnees. Like their chief, Black Hoof, these Shawnees were allies of the United States. In fact, Logan and his group had helped guide Hull and the U.S. army to Detroit. The two met for hours. Despite their friendly discussion, they could not reconcile their very different positions. Tecumseh believed that resisting the United States was the only way Native Americans might preserve their lands and retain their culture. Logan believed that Tecumseh would be destroyed along with the British by the superior force of the United States. They parted sadly, both apparently regretting their inability to agree. Neither man would survive the coming conflict.

Tecumseh continued to send messages and invitations out to other native nations via representatives who carried the symbols of war. One such messenger found the Prophet with a group of Shawnees, Kickapoos, and Winnebagos at Fort Wayne. Tecumseh gave instructions for the Prophet to send the women, children, and elderly away to safety, gather the warriors together, and then strike Vincennes with all of his might. He promised to meet his brother in Winnebago country after the Prophet followed through with this attack. To the south, Tecumseh sent additional communications, calling not only on Native American warriors but also on slaves who wished to escape their bondage. His messages indicated that Great Britain would supply them with arms and ammunition if they fought for the British. After the victorious end of the war, those who were slaves would receive their freedom.

On July 12, Hull's forces crossed over into Canada and seized the settlement of Sandwich, which sat directly north of Amherstburg. This sudden, rather uncontested U.S. victory unnerved some of the late-arriving Native Americans, including Walk-in-the-Water, who promptly returned with his warriors to Brownstown. Despite this setback, Tecumseh managed to dissuade many others from leaving. Matthew Elliott noted that Tecumseh kept most of the American Indians loyal and acted as a great friend and asset to Great Britain because of this. Sandwich was only one small victory. Hull clearly wanted to attack Fort Malden, but he could not transport his artillery to the proper locations. Moreover, he became plagued by indecision and doubts. He worried about his vulnerable communication line. Most important, he feared the Native Americans who had joined forces with the British. His imagination led him to overestimate their numbers wildly and to envision all kinds of savage, unspeakable atrocities that they might commit during a time of war. His fears grew so inflated that they paralyzed him, and his inaction in turn demoralized his men. In this sense, Tecumseh and his warriors played a major role in the conflict simply by being a presence in Canada. But Tecumseh contributed in more ways than this. A series of skirmishes unfolded along the Canard River, which runs between Sandwich and Amherstburg. Tecumseh was known to lead at least one attack on a U.S. reconnaissance patrol, and he probably led several more such ventures, worrying and harassing U.S. soldiers.

On July 17, the most strategic U.S. post in the region, Fort Michilimackinac, fell. A force led by British officers but composed mostly of Native American warriors—warriors who came from native nations brought into the conflict by Tecumseh's efforts—surrounded the fort. Before they could attack, the U.S. soldiers surrendered. This significant loss further rattled Hull. It also induced a number of northern American Indians to join the cause of Tecumseh and the British. The news even had an effect in Brownstown; Tecumseh's fair-weather friend Walk-in-the-Water changed his mind (again) and returned to Fort Malden with his Wyandot warriors. The Native Americans pressed their military and psychological advantages, "haunting" U.S. forces, shadowing them and harrying them when they lacked the numbers to attack. The constant pressure of these guerrilla tactics damaged U.S. resolve.

Tecumseh soon distinguished himself further. He remained in Brownstown after seeing the Wyandots properly escorted to Amherstburg, and he intercepted the news that Hull had sent Major Thomas Van Horne to meet a supply train laden with badly needed provisions and escort it back to Detroit. Tecumseh, who had only 24 warriors with him, sent back to Fort Malden for reinforcements and then laid a trap for Van Horne and his company. The British were too slow in reaching Tecumseh, however, and so the Shawnee chief followed his plan using only the warriors who were with him. Tecumseh ambushed Van Horne. His warriors fought from heavy cover with constant motion in order to disguise their numbers. In the end, Tecumseh's 24 warriors turned back more than 150 U.S. soldiers. The Native Americans lost one comrade while costing the United States eighteen dead and twelve wounded. Van Horne never reached the supply train. It was remarkable victory for Tecumseh, made all the more meaningful when his warriors recovered a mailbag from the debris of battle. They had intercepted a letter from Hull to the secretary of war. In it, Hull explained that his situation was critical. He feared that thousands of American Indians would cut off his position and overwhelm Detroit. To a chief who had just achieved victory against a vastly superior force, the irony of the letter must have been sweet.

Three days later, a larger force of British and Native American men fought the second U.S. detachment sent to retrieve the provisions for Detroit. The resulting Battle of Monguagon technically was a victory for the United States. Many things went wrong during the battle: a separate group of Potawatomis retreated and, in the confusion, became engaged by their own allies; Tecumseh and his party were left to draw all of the U.S. fire when one group of British soldiers mistook the signal for a bayonet charge for a signal to retreat; and Tecumseh was hit by buckshot in the leg, leaving him painfully but not dangerously wounded. U.S. Lieutenant Colonel James Miller and his soldiers won the battle. They were, however, so unnerved by the encounter—and particularly by the fierce fighting of Tecumseh and his warriors, who were the last to retreat from the field—that they refused to go forward to claim the supply train. Miller insisted on receiving reinforcements before he moved. Hull, tortured by his own fears, eventually ordered Miller back to Detroit. They left the supply train to their opponents.

On August 14, Brigadier-General Isaac Brock arrived at Fort Malden. According to eyewitnesses, Brock and Tecumseh liked each other from their very first meeting. Brock was confident and committed, and he assured his American Indian allies that he intended to fight and achieve victory. Tecumseh was clearly grateful that Great Britain had sent a leader who would wage the war wholeheartedly, as if it could be won and was worth winning. Brock expressed his desire to attack Detroit, a plan that Tecumseh strongly supported. Detroit was at its weakest. General Hull feared that the Native Americans occupying Michilimackinac might swoop down on the U.S. forces at Sandwich and overtake them, and so he ordered his men to abandon Sandwich and surrender the territorial advantage that they had gained. His subordinates, frustrated that he would not give the order to attack Amherstburg, conspired to remove him from command. Officials in Ohio confirmed that there were no reinforcements immediately available to send to Detroit. Hull remained paralyzed by doubts and fears, and his soldiers waited in limbo, disheartened and frustrated.

Brock quickly developed deep respect for and trust in Tecumseh, and he seemed to recognize in the Shawnee chief a like mind. Together they devised both a military and a psychological strategy for the assault on Detroit. On August 15, Brock sent a message to Hull demanding the surrender of the settlement. He expected Hull to refuse, and Hull did. Brock took the opportunity of the communication, however, to play upon Hull's worst fears. "It is far from my intention to enter into a war of extermination," Brock wrote, "but you must be aware, that the numerous body of Indians who have attached themselves to my troops will be beyond my control once the contest commences."[5] He left Hull to imagine what horrors might await him. Before Tecumseh and Brock parted, each to lead his own force in the invasion, Brock removed the red sash he wore and gave it to Tecumseh. This token of esteem pleased the Shawnee chief. He later bestowed it on his faithful ally of many years, the Wyandot war chief Roundhead.

Tecumseh now was officially recognized by the British as the military leader of all of the Native Americans. He became known to the whites on both sides of the conflict as the "Indian General." On the night before the attack, Tecumseh moved his warriors into Michigan. There, under cover of darkness, Tecumseh, with the chiefs Roundhead, Main Poc, Walk-in-the-Water, and Splitlog, Matthew Elliott from Amherstburg, and the American Indian army, surrounded the settlement. The following morning was August 16. Brock's troops crossed from Canada and marched on Detroit from the south, while Tecumseh's forces caught the U.S. soldiers by surprise from the north and west. To the east, the British batteries at Sandwich bombarded the fort. As the British advanced, members of the Michigan militia defending Detroit either surrendered or deserted. Hull, who had been contemplating what he believed to be the horrors of American Indian warfare since receiving Brock's letter, was left surrounded by a force nearly double his own and responsible for a settlement full of women, children, and other noncombatants. Shortly after noon, he surrendered. Little did he know that Tecumseh had given his warriors strict instructions to treat all captives as prisoners of war. No soldier or civilian was harmed after the fall of Detroit. All of the prisoners were either paroled or exchanged for British prisoners held by the United States.

In his account of his experiences in Detroit, Robert Wallace, a junior aide to Hull, described being introduced to Tecumseh after the surrender. The meeting impressed him, because he considered Tecumseh to be the greatest general in the land. He recalled that Tecumseh used an interpreter for such interactions, despite the fact he had by this time gained a working knowledge of English. It seems Tecumseh valued courtesy highly and did not wish his imperfect English skills to offend or embarrass. Wallace found him to look imposing, tall and straight and formal, though his speech was kind and reassuring. William Hatch, Hull's assistant quartermaster-general, also met Tecumseh and remembered that he "presented in his appearance and noble bearing one of the finest looking men I have ever seen."[6] Hatch drew a portrait of Tecumseh as being in the prime of his life, which followed a description also related by Captain John B. Glegg, an aide to Brock. Glegg assumed Tecumseh was in his middle thirties, however, when in fact he was a decade older.

Tecumseh was less successful when he and Major Peter Chambers ventured into northwest Ohio to establish control there and take possession of British supplies. At the River Raisin, the British soldiers destroyed U.S. blockhouses, but American Indian warriors pillaged the white settlement. This was not simple lack of discipline; many of the warriors were Wyandots, neighbors of this community, and their anger and frustration after years of hardships were personal and pointed. Tecumseh and Roundhead tried to reestablish order and persuaded some of the marauders to return items they had stolen. Only two lives were lost. Matthew Elliott praised Tecumseh for all he did to keep the situation from growing worse, but Tecumseh was greatly displeased. When the warriors encountered approximately two dozen ill soldiers left by Hull's army at the fortifications on the Maumee River rapids, Tecumseh put these U.S. troops under his personal protection, and no one challenged their safety.

On August 15, Potawatomi warriors attacked the U.S. garrison from Fort Dearborn. They killed more than half of the soldiers in battle and then took the remainder as prisoners, securing the fort for Tecumseh's confederacy and the British. On the whole, the Native American forces achieved remarkable victories, often while fighting forces of superior size and arms. In six weeks, the American Indians and the British had destroyed or taken control of all U.S. posts west of Cleveland on the upper Great Lakes and effectively ended the U.S. invasion of Canada. General Brock repeatedly praised the heroism of his Native American allies and became one of many who called Tecumseh "the Wellington of the Indians."

Before he returned east, Brock spoke at some length with Tecumseh. He then wrote a letter to the new British prime minister, Lord Liverpool, in which he discussed his ally: "He who attracted most of my attention was a Shawnee chief, Tecumset, brother to the Prophet, who for the last two years has carried on (contrary to our remonstrances) an Active Warfare against the United States—a more sagacious or more a gallant Warrior does not I believe exist. He was the admiration of every one who conversed with him." Brock explained what he had learned from Tecumseh about how the United States "corrupted a few dissolute characters whom they pretended to consider as chiefs and with whom they contracted engagements and concluded Treaties, which they have attempted to impose on the whole Indian race."[7] He noted that the British would claim Native American loyalty if they could include American Indians in the final negotiations for peace when the war ended, and he urged that the British recognize Native American rights to the land taken from them.

With a pan-tribal army at his back and a powerful ally who supported his goal of reclaiming Native American lands, Tecumseh had never been closer to achieving all he had hoped for his people.

NOTES

1. John D. Hunter, *Memoirs of a Captivity among the Indians of North America*, 3rd ed. (London: n.p., 1824), pp. 43–48.

2. Quoted in "Documents, Artefacts and Imagery," *Military Subjects: War of 1812 Magazine*, Issue 2 (February 2006). Available at http://www.napoleon-series. org/military/Warof1812/2006/Issue2/c_abos.html. Also quoted in C. F. Klinck, ed., *Tecumseh: Fact and Fiction in Early Records* (Ottawa: Tecumseh Press, 1978), p. 125.

3. Ibid.

4. Ibid., pp. 125–126.

5. Quoted in R. David Edmunds, *Tecumseh and the Quest for Indian Leadership* (New York: Longman, 1984), p. 179.

6. Quoted in John Sudgen, *Tecumseh: A Life* (New York: Henry Holt, 1997), p. 307.

7. Quoted in C. F. Klinck, ed., *Tecumseh: Fact and Fiction in Early Records* (Ottawa: Tecumseh Press, 1978), p. 141.

Chapter 8

THE BATTLE OF THE THAMES

Just as Tecumseh's goals seemed nearly within reach, everything changed. Brock went east to the Niagara frontier to prepare for an expected U.S. invasion. His successor, Major-General Henry Procter, was equally aware of how indispensable Tecumseh and his forces were to the British cause. Unfortunately, Procter was neither as bold nor as gifted as Brock, and he never achieved the same relationship Brock had enjoyed with the American Indian allies. Almost immediately, the fortunes of war seemed to turn. On September 5, Potawatomi warriors surrounded and attacked Fort Wayne. The U.S. soldiers trapped within the stockade refused to surrender, and the warriors appealed to Canada with requests for additional men and arms. Major Adam Muir and Tecumseh left Amherstburg with a force of more than a thousand men, well over half of whom were American Indian warriors. Before they could join the attack, however, they learned that William Henry Harrison and an army of over two thousand had gone to Fort Wayne's assistance. The Potawatomis retreated.

Harrison's soldiers continued on toward the British-Native American force. Muir and Tecumseh agreed that they should stay and fight. They prepared for battle above the mouth of the Auglaize on September 26, but General James Winchester, who now commanded the U.S. soldiers, received information about his waiting opponents and slowed his pace. Muir feared the army might move in the night and so retreated downstream. Some of the warriors scattered during the retreat, and Tecumseh set off after them to persuade them to return. The following day, against the advice of Roundhead, Muir retreated yet again. His indecision frustrated the American Indians still more, especially the Ottawas and the Chippewas from the Michilimackinac region, who left and returned to Canada. Tecumseh and Roundhead talked with Muir long into the night, assuring him that the other warriors would remain and that they could still defeat their opponent, but Muir's fears increased. With Harrison's men only two miles away, Muir called off the engagement altogether and ordered a full retreat. Tecumseh was disheartened by the orders, and especially by the lack of decisive leadership he saw from both Muir and Procter.

Rumor at the time and sensationalist reports after the fact almost certainly exaggerated the tensions between Tecumseh and Procter. Although they at times disagreed vehemently, there was no indication from either that personal animosity was involved. In fact, the opposite was true. Procter always referred to Tecumseh in his writings and speeches with respect and admiration. Tecumseh often dined with Procter and his family, sharing conversation and jokes with Procter's children and guests. Although he attended war dances and fought in war paint, as his fellow Native Americans did, Tecumseh also took great pains to accommodate his ally's culture, including the social expectations that came with it. One description, by the French Canadian Thomas Vercheres de Boucherville, who often accompanied Tecumseh while the Shawnee chief was in Canada, described Tecumseh at a banquet: "Tecumseh was seated at my left with his pistols on either side of his plate and his big hunting knife in front.... He wore a red cloak, trousers of deerskin, and a printed calico shirt, the whole outfit a present from the English. His bearing was irreproachable for a man of the woods as he was, much better than that of some so-called gentlemen."[1] After Tecumseh's death, Procter's son-in-law recounted family memories of the chief and the manner in which he socialized with the English, saying he "readily and cheerfully accommodated himself to all the novelties of his situation, and seemed amused, without being at all embarrassed by them."[2]

Disagreements between Tecumseh and Procter, when not about military strategy, often were based on principle, not personality. For example, Procter took his duty to protect the military secrets of the British-Native American alliance very seriously. He feared that spies were leaking information to the U.S. forces. One of the ways he combated this was to enforce martial law on the city of Detroit and to institute other practices—administering oaths of allegiance or neutrality, detaining suspects, and sometimes sending them east for further examination—that severely infringed on the liberty of the citizens. Tecumseh at times argued on behalf of the civilian population. One classic example involved Father Gabriel Richard, of Saint Anne's Church in Detroit. Before the war even began, Richard was famous for his work in educating American Indians and disadvantaged whites in the region. After the fall of Detroit, Richard encouraged the town's inhabitants to remain loyal to the United States, and Procter had the priest imprisoned. Tecumseh interceded on Richard's behalf and gained his freedom. He did not confine his concern to friends of Native America, either; another often-repeated story is that Tecumseh reproached one of the British staff of the Indian Department, because the Shawnee had learned that this man had abused his wife.

Tecumseh was a diplomat as well as a warrior. Unlike his brother the Prophet, for example, he understood the importance of symbolic action, but he also knew when it was best to compromise. The Shawnee chief politely declined every offer of alcohol but proved willing to wear Anglo fashions and attend formal British functions, and he apparently fit in very well when he wished to do so. He could show true humility to "elder brother" native nations such as the Wyandots, aware of his place as a "younger sibling" Shawnee, and yet present himself as the spokesman for all of Native America when negotiating with the United States or Great Britain. Suggestions of a clash of personalities do not fit what we know of Tecumseh or the evidence left by Procter. But genuine disagreements did occur, far more often than they had with General Brock. Procter lacked many of the personal and professional attributes that had made Brock Tecumseh's close ally and friend.

On October 13, Tecumseh learned that Brock had been killed in the Battle of Queenston Heights while leading a counterattack against U.S. forces. Tecumseh was deeply shaken by the loss of the one British official he had known who had never betrayed his trust or confidence. This news, coupled with the recent failed attempt to engage Harrison's forces, represented a stark and sobering contrast to previous successes. Two months later, with winter in full force, visitors took Amherstburg and Tecumseh by surprise. The Prophet and his people appeared, bedraggled and in need of shelter and food. The Prophet had not attacked Vincennes as instructed. Instead, he had followed his own ill-conceived strategy and attacked Fort Harrison in present-day Terre Haute. The Prophetstown force, mostly made up of Winnebagos and Kickapoos, first tried to enter the fort by trickery. When this failed, they burned the stockade and opened fire on the garrison. Captain Zachary Taylor, a future president of the United States, saved the stockade and drove back the attackers. Some returned to the Prophetstown area, while others rode south and killed several white settlers in retaliation for their humiliation.

The Prophet, embarrassed yet again, worried about U.S. reprisals against his community. He grew increasingly concerned after the failed attack on Fort Wayne by the Potawatomis. After William Henry Harrison reinforced Fort Wayne, he sent his troops across the northeastern region of the territory, laying waste to American Indian villages and crops. The Prophet hid much of the provisions meant to sustain those in the Prophetstown area and moved his people into the swamps to hide. In mid-November, the Kentucky militia destroyed the Native American villages on the Wabash River near the mouth of the Tippecanoe. The soldiers also scoured the woods; there they found the food and supplies that the refugees had hidden, which they confiscated. Once again, the Prophet and his people were without shelter and food, facing a harsh winter. Small parties of warriors managed to kill more than a dozen of the Kentuckians, but they lacked the numbers and the heart for a larger conflict. In despair, the Prophet and the remnants of Prophetstown made the trek to Canada to ask for assistance from Tecumseh and the British.

The Prophet's appearance was problematic for Tecumseh for two reasons. First, it proved that part of Tecumseh's plans for Indiana territory had failed because of the Prophet's poor judgment. Second, the Prophet requested what Tecumseh could not give. Even the impressive stores of Fort Malden could not possibly feed throughout the winter all of the American Indian warriors who had come to Amherstburg to fight. Procter and Tecumseh agreed that the warriors who could return to their home villages—those from northern Indiana and southern Michigan, for example—should take what provisions they needed for their journey and then return home to hunt during the coldest months. Tecumseh planned to go with them and then bring them back to Fort Malden for a spring offensive against the United States. The Prophet came seeking protection and food, just as Tecumseh was leaving with his warriors to find the same thing. Unwilling to cross Tecumseh after once again disappointing him, the Prophet retraced his steps and followed his brother back into Indiana.

While wintering with allies such as Main Poc, Tecumseh learned more about how his message had influenced the south. There was distressing news from the Creek nation. Tecumseh must have been upset to hear that some of the Creeks who once had followed him had murdered white settlers and then in turn been killed by fellow Creeks. The widening schism between the Upper and the Lower Creeks promised continued intratribal bloodshed, a result directly opposite to the unity Tecumseh had hoped to promote. All of the news from the Creek nation was not bad, however. A Creek war party promised to come north and fight beside Tecumseh in the late spring.

It seems Tecumseh's message also yielded fruit as far away as Florida. The United States was trying to annex part of Florida from Spain by force and had the Spanish governor, Sebastian Kindelan, surrounded in St. Augustine. In July 1812, a group of Seminoles, runaway slaves, and so-called black Seminoles allied with Spain against the United States. The inspiration behind their struggle was the guide and interpreter Tecumseh had left among the Creeks and some of the Red Stick Creeks who followed him. Together, they brought Tecumseh's message to the Seminoles, and the resulting conflict continued to unfold in Florida among people who had never seen Tecumseh in person but knew his ideas by heart. Eventually, the United States invaded the Native regions of Florida, destroying Seminole villages and forcing the flight of the American Indians, blacks, and mixed-bloods. Their resistance movement continued even after the U.S. annexation of Florida, however, leading arguably to the most successful slave revolt in U.S. history, as well as to an ongoing pattern of Native American resistance followed for generations. Tecumseh did not live to see the effects his ideas produced in Florida, but he must have appreciated knowing that yet another native nation was resisting the United States in the spirit of his confederacy.

Tecumseh had not yet returned to Canada when the British won a remarkable, if not altogether satisfying, victory. William Henry Harrison, now in command of the Army of the Northwest, attempted to retake Detroit. He divided his force into two columns, leading one himself and putting the other under the command of General James Winchester. Winchester disobeyed Harrison's orders, moving far ahead of Harrison's column and capturing the Canadian settlement of Frenchtown. Winchester invaded and subdued Frenchtown easily, but on January 22, 1823, Procter and Roundhead counterattacked and defeated the U.S. forces. Winchester himself was captured. He agreed to surrender if Procter gave his word that the U.S. prisoners would be safe. Procter did so. Thus, with the Battle of Frenchtown, Harrison's plans for liberating Detroit died. But the victory was not entirely sweet. Procter promised that the U.S. prisoners would be protected, but he lacked enough sleighs to carry the wounded, and so he left them unguarded in Frenchtown to be transported the following day. A small party of drunken Native American warriors came upon the defenseless soldiers and killed them. This became known as the Raisin River Massacre and gave U.S. soldiers "Remember the Raisin!" as a battle cry throughout the rest of the war. Historians estimate that, between the battle and the murders, nearly three hundred U.S. soldiers were killed and nearly double that number were captured.

The news of American Indian atrocities was bitter to Tecumseh. He encouraged his followers to abstain, as he did, from alcohol; these warriors had been inebriated. He instructed his followers to treat all captives as prisoners of war, with mercy and respect; these warriors had butchered those who could not protect themselves. Procter added insult to the situation by blaming the warriors entirely, even though he was the one who failed to provide guards for the prisoners. Despite the unfortunate murders, however, the Battle of Frenchtown was a welcome victory for the British and Native Americans. More warriors from northern native nations appeared in Amherstburg, ready to fight the United States.

On April 16, Tecumseh returned to Fort Malden and brought hundreds of warriors with him. In the same month, Harrison and his U.S. forces completed a new post, Fort Meigs, near the current town of Maumee, Ohio. From this position, Harrison planned to liberate Detroit and invade Canada. Procter was anxious to attack Fort Meigs before Harrison could receive additional reinforcements. On April 24, Tecumseh and approximately twelve hundred Native American warriors set off on foot around the western end of Lake Erie, bound for the Maumee. At Swan Creek, they rendezvoused with Procter, whose British troops, artillery, and gunboats had traveled by water. Together, they had the U.S. fort both outmanned and outgunned. By May 1, the soldiers had installed heavy artillery on two batteries, one across from Fort Meigs and one on a hill above it. While the British forces were moving guns into position, the Native Americans were busy, as well. One party of Winnebagos and Kickapoos attacked the animals kept beneath the walls of the fort, chasing away the horses and killing the livestock. A group of Ottawa boys—the eldest was 14—ambushed U.S. soldiers with dispatches from the Sandusky region. The troops fled, leaving their documents behind for their enemies. These small achievements had a significant impact on morale for both the American Indian warriors and the British forces.

Within the stockade, Harrison hid the movements of his men behind a row of tents. He ordered them to construct earthen walls and trenches across the grounds, designed to limit the damage any bombs or shells could inflict. When the British and Native Americans attacked, they discovered the earthworks and their effectiveness. For four days they wasted ammunition on the fort without accomplishing much at all. Procter called for Harrison's surrender. Harrison replied that, if Procter could take the fort, it would bring him far more honor than if Harrison had surrendered one hundred times. Harrison had well-constructed defenses and more reinforcements on their way; he did not think Procter could capture Fort Meigs. He was correct.

The U.S. reinforcements, General Green Clay and his Kentucky militia, arrived and attacked the unsuspecting British and Native Americans on May 5. They captured the British cannons and scattered the soldiers and warriors who were protecting them. The American Indian warriors fled toward their camp, and the Kentuckians followed. Tecumseh and Major Adam Muir quickly organized their men at the camp and rushed forward to engage the militia. The Kentuckians were wholly unprepared for this offensive. Some panicked, threw aside their weapons, and headed for the river. When they reached the water, they found that other British and American Indian forces had not only retaken the cannons but also captured the U.S. boats. Of the 800 Kentuckians who had come to Harrison's defense, only about 150 ever made it to Fort Meigs.

A combination of British and American Indian forces moved the U.S. prisoners nearby to the ruins of Fort Miami, near the Native American encampment. En route the warriors harassed their captives, stripping them and stealing their personal effects. Once they arrived at Fort Miami, the Natives formed two rows leading to the gates and forced the U.S. soldiers to run the gauntlet, facing muskets, tomahawks, clubs, and other weapons in the process. Once the prisoners who survived the gauntlet entered the fort, they faced death again. Some of the Native American warriors followed them into the holding area and began killing the militiamen. One warrior even shot an aged British soldier who tried to protect the prisoners. The accounts of witnesses describe an ugly scene of violence against men, many of them wounded, who could not protect themselves. Some of the British did try, albeit rather feebly, to end the rampage, but they met no success.

The moment Tecumseh learned of the killing, he and Matthew Elliott raced to the fort. They found approximately forty Kentuckians dead and the atrocities still under way. According to the recollections of some of the survivors, Tecumseh's appearance immediately ended the killing. They remembered Tecumseh storming into the fort, climbing onto one of the walls so that he could be easily seen and heard, and making an impassioned speech to the warriors. It is possible that some of the angry Ojibwes and Potawatomis who were responsible for the carnage did not understand his words any better than the Kentuckians did, without the assistance of a translator, but his meaning was obvious, nonetheless. The shamed warriors apparently left as quickly as possible. Tecumseh then turned his anger on the British who had watched the bloodshed and done little, if anything, to stop it.

The letters and memoirs of the survivors recalled Tecumseh's defense in grateful, glowing terms; all recognized that they owed their lives to the Shawnee chief's mercy. It is difficult to determine which of the descriptions include romantic embellishments, especially since the entire event was kept as quiet as possible in the official British dispatches. Some claimed that Tecumseh waved a sword and said that only cowards killed unarmed prisoners. Others said that he brandished a tomahawk and dared anyone to try to harm another captive. All agree, however, that he appeared as a commanding, forceful presence, terrible in his anger and gentle in his mercy. One detail that appears in several records and is often retold in biographical accounts of the Shawnee chief cannot be verified, but it speaks to the legend as much as to the man. After calling the American Indian murderers and torturers disgraceful, Tecumseh accused the British of watching the slaughter, saying, "I conquer to save, and you to murder!" or some variation of the sentiment. Perhaps this tells us more about how the survivors saw and appreciated Tecumseh than about what the chief actually said. Regardless of its veracity, it is a telling anecdote.

Popular accounts of Tecumseh's honor and compassion often focus on this incident. Fewer point out the event that followed. Matthew Elliott informed Tecumseh that four other prisoners were taken during the battle and were being held by the Wyandots. Tecumseh found them and immediately knew why they had been separated from the U.S. soldiers; these were Shawnees from Ohio who had sided with and fought for the United States. The Wyandots had stripped, beaten, and tortured them. Tecumseh unbound and greeted them and then told the Wyandots—and the Potawatomis and others—that they were not to be harmed. He asked each of the prisoners to pledge not to run, and they did so. He then put them under the protection of two warriors whom he trusted fully. He promised the captives that he would call a council, create a message for Black Hoof, and then send them back with it. On May 14, they were escorted home to Ohio. Tecumseh kept his word. He had treated them with mercy and respect, despite the fact he could easily have interpreted their efforts against his confederacy as a betrayal. Although they worked directly against his efforts and hopes for all Shawnees and all Native Americans, he gave them every courtesy. This was, however, completely consistent for Tecumseh. He understood cruelty to be beneath an honorable Shawnee warrior and man; moreover, he despised intertribal violence and wanted nothing more than unity among the native nations.

The first Battle of Fort Meigs was neither the victory the British and American Indians had hoped for nor the defeat Harrison had expected for them. The U.S. forces remained at Fort Meigs, but the battle effectively rendered the post harmless. The British and Native Americans, although they did not achieve their original objective, suffered a fraction of the losses their opponent did and possessed captured boats filled with welcome supplies. Tecumseh returned to Amherstburg with his warriors—and the Prophet, who had watched the action from a safe distance. The following weeks were unsatisfying for Tecumseh. He and some of his forces built a village on the Huron River south of Detroit, where they could defend the Canadian border from U.S. forces. Tecumseh and his warriors were in the war not to defend Canada, however, but to restore their lands. The Shawnee chief expressed his concern to Procter: he needed victories soon, not a long and painful stalemate, if the native nations were to have enough leverage at the end of the war to demand the return of their property. When almost six hundred warriors from western native nations appeared at Fort Malden, eager to join the conflict, Tecumseh knew that some action had to be taken, or the new recruits would grow bored, lose heart, and abandon the cause.

Tecumseh persuaded Procter to try once more to capture Fort Meigs. In mid-July, the British and the Native Americans set a trap for General Green Clay, who now commanded the fort, and his soldiers. They attempted to draw the U.S. force out of the stockade by convincing them that their reinforcements were under attack nearby. This involved an elaborate and clever mock battle orchestrated by Tecumseh to simulate a bloody conflict. The charade convinced U.S. soldiers, who pleaded with Clay to be allowed to help their comrades, but Clay knew better. Unknown to Tecumseh, a U.S. messenger had managed to enter the fort with communications for Clay that proved that no reinforcements were close enough to be fighting enemy forces. Clay knew he was being tricked. At last Tecumseh and his warriors withdrew, badly disappointed. They attacked the small Fort Stephenson on the Sandusky River in a desperate attempt to reverse their fortunes and revive morale. This time, the British proved gullible. Believing when they met no defense that the U.S. forces were preoccupied with fighting Tecumseh and his warriors, Procter advanced his soldiers. The U.S. soldiers waited until the British were in the clear, attempting a frontal assault, trapped in the dry moat right beneath their enemies, and then opened fire. The British losses were so high that not enough men were left to sail all of the gunboats back to Canada.

Demoralized after two successive defeats, many Sacs, Foxes, Menominees, and Chippewas deserted. Others joined the United States. Harrison sensed an opportunity to drive a wedge between the British and the American Indians and sent the Brownstown Wyandots an invitation to make peace. When his messengers arrived in Brownstown, they found Tecumseh, the Prophet, Roundhead, and Matthew Elliott waiting for them there. Nonetheless, Harrison's representatives relayed his offer. He explained that the U.S. Navy would soon be on Lake Erie. He expected this would be news to the Wyandots, because, he alleged, the British had kept information from them, including important news about recent defeats that had drastically weakened the British position in Upper Canada. Harrison reminded the Wyandots that Procter and Tecumseh had failed to capture U.S. posts in Ohio; they certainly could not take on the U.S. Navy. He extended the hand of friendship to the Wyandots and hoped they would join him as allies.

Roundhead, Tecumseh, and Elliott took the opportunity to rebut Harrison and exhort the Wyandots to remain loyal to the confederacy and the British. After they left Brownstown, however, Walk-in-the-Water, always ready to support the stronger side of a conflict, told his people that he planned to change his allegiance once again. The Wyandot case was unusual, but it was also a symptom of a larger disillusionment that plagued a good number of the Native American warriors. They sensed fear in Procter's unwillingness to commit his full resources to offensives. This pattern continued. When Captain Oliver H. Perry appeared with the fledgling U.S. fleet at the mouth of the Detroit River, Tecumseh and his warriors could not understand why Captain Robert H. Barclay did not respond with the British fleet immediately.

When the British finally did challenge U.S. naval power on Lake Erie, in September 1813, however, the U.S. forces either sank or captured every ship in the entire British fleet. Procter called for a formal council at Amherstburg and, on September 18, told Tecumseh and the rest of the Native Americans of the overwhelming U.S. naval victory. He explained that this spectacular defeat changed the entire course of the war. He planned to abandon Detroit, Sandwich, and Amherstburg and fall back to the Niagara frontier. There he would join with other British forces. He asked his American Indian allies to go with him. There, he promised, they would receive plenty of supplies and be of tremendous help in the defense of Canada.

The fact that Procter assumed the Native Americans would easily desert the region or would consider defending Canada their primary purpose proved that he did not understand fully why the American Indians were in Amherstburg and what they were fighting to achieve. The English translation of Tecumseh's response—one of the most famous speeches in Native American history—was preserved by the Canadian government and eventually used as evidence in the court martial of Henry Procter. Various witnesses described Tecumseh at the council. He wore a buckskin suit and an ostrich plume in his hair. After Procter delivered his announcement,

Tecumseh stood, holding a wampum belt in his hands, and replied directly to the major-general:

> Father! Listen to your children; you see them now all before you. The war before this [the Revolutionary War] our British Father gave the hatchet to his red children, when our old chiefs were alive. They are now all dead. In that war our Father was thrown on his back by the Americans, and our Father took them by the hand without our knowledge, and we are afraid our Father will do so again at this time. Summer before last, when I came forward with my red children, and was ready to take up the hatchet in favour of our British Father, we were told not to be in a hurry—that he had not yet determined to fight the Americans.
>
> Listen! When war was declared, our Father stood up and gave us the tomahawk, and told us he was now ready to strike the Americans, that he wanted our assistance; and that he certainly would get us our lands back which the Americans had taken from us.
>
> Listen! You told us at that time to bring forward our families to this place. We did so, and you promised to take care of them, and that they should want for nothing, while the men would go to fight the enemy—that we were not to trouble ourselves with the enemy's garrisons—that we knew nothing about them, and that our Father would attend to that part of the business. You also told your red children that you would take care of your garrison here which made our hearts glad.
>
> Listen! When we last went to the Rapids [Fort Meigs], it is true that we gave you little assistance. It is hard to fight people who live like ground hogs.
>
> Father listen! Our fleet has gone out, we know they have fought; we have heard the great guns; but know nothing of what has happened to our Father with one Arm [Captain Robert Barclay]. Our ships have gone one way, and we are much astonished to see our Father tying up every thing and preparing to run the other way, without letting his red children know what his intentions are. You always told us to remain here and take care of our lands; it made our hearts glad to hear that was your wish. Our Great Father, the King, is the head and you represent him. You always told us that you would never draw your foot off British ground; but now, Father, we see you

are drawing back, and we are sorry to see our Father doing so, without seeing the enemy. We must compare our Father's conduct to a fat animal that carries its tail upon its back; but when affrighted, it drops it between its legs and runs off.

Listen Father! The Americans have not yet defeated us by land; neither are we sure that they have done so by water; we therefore wish to remain here, and fight our enemy should they make their appearance. If they defeat us, we will then retreat with our Father. At the battle of the Rapids last war the American certainly defeated us; and when we retreated to our Father's fort at that place the gates were shut against us. We were afraid that it would now be the case; but instead of that we now see our British Father preparing to march out of his garrison.

Father! You have got the arms and ammunition which our Great Father [the King] sent for his red children. If you have an idea of going away, give them to us, and you may go and welcome for us. Our lives are in the hands of the Great Spirit. We are determined to defend our lands, and if it is his will, we wish to leave our bones upon them.[3]

After Tecumseh finished, the American Indians erupted in cheers and war cries, while Procter sat mute, stunned by what he had heard. After Matthew Elliott managed to restore some order to the council, Procter asked if Tecumseh would meet him again in three days so that he could respond to the Shawnee chief's comments. Tecumseh agreed. Procter and Elliott discussed the situation for the next three days. Elliott was worried that if Procter continued with his plan, the warriors would either depart for Michigan, leaving the British badly outnumbered, or, worse yet, join the United States and fight against the British. On September 21, Procter suggested a compromise to Tecumseh. He explained that they were particularly vulnerable in the Detroit area to the now-uncontested U.S. Navy, which could cut off their supplies and communications easily. Rather than fall back as far as he had originally planned, he asked if Tecumseh and his warriors would retreat with him to Chatham on the Thames River, which was far upstream and thus not threatened by U.S. ships. There they could gather their forces, restock on supplies, and prepare to make a stand against Harrison and the Long Knives. After consideration, Tecumseh agreed.

Many American Indians did not like the compromise. In the end, Main Poc led a force of Chippewas, Foxes, Ottawas, Potawatomis, and Sacs to Michigan. There they plundered U.S. property and awaited the outcome of the confrontation. They planned to fall on retreating U.S. forces if Tecumseh and Procter succeeded, but they had no desire to move further from their homes and risk everything for the British cause alone. Approximately three thousand Native Americans, including women and children, moved toward the Thames with the British. Many were personally loyal to Tecumseh, family and friends who had followed him for years, such as his sister, Tecumapease, and her husband, Wahsikegaboe, and Tecumseh's son, Paukeesaa, whom they had raised. Tecumseh remained in Amherstburg with Matthew Elliott, whose life had been tied to the Shawnees for the past 40 years. Together, the two waited until they saw Harrison's forces land and begin to occupy the village. They were the very last to leave.

On October 1, Tecumseh and Elliott reached the mouth of the Thames only to learn distressing news. First, almost half of the three thousand American Indians who had begun the retreat changed their minds en route, abandoning the British and altering their course for Michigan. This was a terrible blow to the entire endeavor. But there was one other loss that probably affected Tecumseh even more. He learned that his long-time ally and friend, Chief Roundhead, had been killed while scouting the movements of Harrison's army. Tecumseh's world seemed to be crumbling all around him. The next day brought him to Chatham and yet more disappointment. The Native Americans camped on the south shore of the river, but the British moved north, above it. The two groups were separated, not working together, and few preparations had been made for facing Harrison's troops. The soldiers and warriors had created no earthworks, formed no defensible camp structure. Procter, in fact, was not even present. Tecumseh was furious. According to reports, he chided the American Indians for wasting precious time and then accused the British soldiers of cowardice. He demanded that the British cross the river and help the warriors prepare for Harrison's army. They refused, saying they had no boats. Two days later, Procter sent word that he had found a more defensible spot upriver, just below Moraviantown. Tecumseh and the Native Americans had no choice but to follow the British army there.

Once again, Tecumseh hung back to wait for Harrison's army. The retreat of the Native American warriors and their families was slow, and Tecumseh wished to buy as much time as possible for his people to get to Moraviantown. A select group of warriors remained with him. They destroyed two bridges spanning McGregor's Creek, which the U.S. soldiers would attempt to cross, and there they planned an ambush. The resulting skirmish was brief—Harrison trained his artillery on the warriors, who were grossly outnumbered—but it slowed Harrison's advance. Tecumseh spent the night at the mill of a local farmer, in part to protect the home from any warriors who might try to vent their frustration on a defenseless white settler. On the next morning, October 5, 1813, Tecumseh waited until he saw the approaching enemy army before he left, bringing up the rear of his own forces, watching to make certain everyone retreated safely. He then rode hard for the site where the combined British and Native American forces would make their stand. He found them two miles west of Moraviantown.

When Tecumseh at last caught up to Procter, he must have been reminded of General Hull at Detroit, paralyzed by indecision and fear, making one mistake after another in the frantic attempt to avoid making any. Up until the last possible moment, Procter was considering yet another spot as a better setting for the confrontation. His troops were exhausted after being lined up and prepared for battle and then forced to relocate, only to go through the same process again. They were hungry and low on ammunition, as well. Procter's artillery and resources, like the Native Americans' food and supplies, were scattered across several miles and falling one after the other into U.S. hands as the invading army advanced. The warriors, increasingly uncertain of their British allies and unwilling to commit suicide for the Canadian cause, had continued to defect. On that day, approximately 450 British and 500 Native Americans—Creeks, Delawares, Foxes, Kickapoos, Ojibwes, Ottawas, Potawatomis, Sacs, Shawnees, Winnebagos, and Wyandots, as well as some "white Indians"—took the field. Harrison's army outnumbered them three to one.

The British formed two lines in an open field, with no breastworks or cover for protection. Tecumseh's warriors formed another line to their right, hidden in the woods of a marshy thicket between two patches of swamp. Together, Procter and Tecumseh, with Elliott as translator, discussed the battle plan and reviewed the troops. Then Tecumseh took his place among his people and waited. Once more, legend, memory, and truth are difficult to disentangle; popular oral traditions, as well as a number of accounts recorded after the fact—in some cases, a significant number of years after the fact—suggest that Tecumseh experienced a foreshadowing of his own death, much as his brother Cheeseekau reportedly had. Witnesses remember him as acting particularly thoughtful but neither grieved nor frightened. Then again, a rather weary fatalism apparently affected many of the warriors at the scene, and this is not surprising, considering the haphazard events and disheartening frustrations of the weeks prior to the battle. Some sources suggest that Tecumseh entrusted his sword to friends with the request that they give it to his son if he grew to be a good warrior. What is certain is that Tecumseh spoke encouragingly to British soldiers and Native warriors alike and then prepared to stand firm against his opponent.

The army arrived in midafternoon. Harrison ordered his soldiers to attack the British first in a charge of mounted militia and ground forces, concentrated on the six-pounder Procter had set up at the center of the main road, the only cannon the British had placed in position for the battle. When the U.S. forces charged, the British crew minding the six-pounder ran from the charge so quickly that they forgot to fire the weapon. The other British soldiers discharged a few halfhearted shots and then abandoned their lines. The entire British effort in the Battle of the Thames lasted five minutes at the most. The British cost the U.S. forces only one casualty. Most of the British soldiers believed the fight was a lost cause even before it began. Procter made an attempt to rally his men and reform the collapsed lines, and then he turned and rode hard for Moraviantown, soon outdistancing his retreating men. Tecumseh and his warriors were left to face the U.S. army alone.

There was no question what would happen next. Tecumseh was determined to fight, even if he had been abandoned by his allies. He was accustomed to outrageous odds. His warriors held fast; some even advanced from their sheltered positions to push the British back along the road. But U.S. Colonel Richard M. Johnson turned his mounted militia into the woods, crowding the warriors and pouring fire into the thick underbrush. The U.S. infantry units advanced, as well, and added their firepower. The American Indians fought valiantly for a time. During the close combat, Tecumseh fell, mortally wounded. As the warriors realized that their leader was dead, they pulled back and fled, utterly demoralized and defeated. The Battle of the Thames lasted only half an hour, and yet it brought the death not only of the Shawnee chief Tecumseh but also of the Native American alliance with Great Britain and of Tecumseh's pan-tribal confederacy.

Two mysteries in particular remain about Tecumseh's death: the identity of his killer and the location of his body. Both were the subject of intense debate in the days and years following the Battle of the Thames, and they continue to be argued today. Many of the missing aspects of Tecumseh's early life are unknown because of a lack of sources and records. The opposite is true in these cases; vast numbers of interviews, letters, memoirs, and articles exist from those who were there—or claimed to be there—at Tecumseh's death or burial or both, but, unfortunately, many of them are quite contradictory. It seems probable that neither of the mysteries will ever be satisfactorily resolved. Colonel Richard Johnson claimed to be the one who shot Tecumseh when he led the cavalry charge into the woods where Tecumseh had organized his warriors. Others corroborated this story, but their motives might not all have been the same. Some Native Americans suggested that no mere soldier could have vanquished their leader; perhaps casting Johnson as the killer gave an added dignity to the slain chief's death. Johnson was also a politically powerful man. He had already served in the Kentucky House of Representatives, and his career took him all the way to the vice presidency; perhaps some individuals from the United States agreed with his account to support him or because they did not wish to cross him. Regardless, his claim was challenged by others with equally vivid accounts of Tecumseh's death, and the question of who actually killed the Shawnee leader remains unanswered.

The final resting place of Tecumseh's body is another mystery that will probably always lack resolution. The Native American warriors withdrew from the close fighting in the thicket and swamps too quickly to bring their dead with them. They returned only after the British had left the field. Both Ohio Shawnees who fought with the U.S. forces and British prisoners recognized the dead body, but William Henry Harrison never made a formal identification. The U.S. soldiers desecrated some of the bodies left at the battle site. There are conflicting accounts about whether a warrior's body, mutilated, skinned, and scalped, belonged to Tecumseh or another man who was mistaken for him. Many of those who carried away the grisly trophies from the corpse later claimed to possess leathery strips of the leader's flesh, but they could not prove it. Conversely, some of those who followed Tecumseh claimed that his body was not violated and that they buried it secretly so that it would remain unmolested. In the most recent historical study of the question of Tecumseh's final resting place, the award-winning 2006 book *Tecumseh's Bones*, the author Guy St-Denis explored a number of potential possibilities. He ultimately determined that Tecumseh most likely was buried where he fell, dug up again unintentionally by a farmer, and reburied in a location that is now lost to the ages.

The years dealt unkindly with many of the leading figures in Tecumseh's life. Sir George Prevost invited Tecumseh's sister, Tecumapease, who had lost both her husband and her brother in the war, to Quebec, where he honored her with a speech and condolence gifts. In 1815, she accepted the fifty-dollar compensation the British offered to American Indian widows whose husbands were killed while fighting for the British. She died shortly thereafter. Tecumseh's son, Paukeesaa, with whom he had never been close, was the overwhelmingly popular choice to be the civil chief of the Shawnees at Lake Ontario, although he was only a teenager. After the war, the young man surrendered his position willingly. He remained with his people, returning to Ohio and then emigrating to Kansas with other Shawnees. Accounts suggest he might have attended an intertribal conference hosted by the Cherokees in Tahlequah, Indian Territory, in 1843. There is some disagreement among historians on the question of whether the Shawnee chief "Big Jim," who was born in Texas in 1834, was the son of Paukeesaa. He was apparently recognized throughout the region as Tecumseh's grandson. He led a group called the Absentee Shawnees and was known for resisting Christianity and resenting the encroachment of white settlers. He died of smallpox in 1900 while in Mexico, investigating locations where he might relocate his people to escape the expansion of the United States.

The Prophet fled with the British at the Battle of the Thames and thus was not present at his brother's death. He continued to serve as a chief of sorts during the war, but, after the Treaty of Ghent, he was treated as more of a nuisance than a leader by most British and American Indians alike. Some Shawnees and Kickapoos from Prophetstown continued to remain with him for some time out of loyalty. The Prophet stayed in Canada for some years but eventually returned to the United States to help the Shawnees emigrate west. His community built a village on the site of present-day Kansas City, Kansas. Slowly the Prophet became simply Tenskwatawa, a man who grew increasingly morose and frustrated as he aged and who turned again to alcohol as he had as a youth. He told long and increasingly embellished stories of his brother and their past together and spent significant time imagining what Tecumseh might have accomplished if he had lived. Tenskwatawa died in 1836.

Henry Procter was court-martialed in the winter of 1814–1815 and found to be deficient in the judgment he used and the energy he showed during the war. His punishment was a public reprimand and suspension from rank and pay for six months. Although his suspension was later rescinded, he never worked again. He died in 1822, in Bath, England.

The Battle of the Thames was an overwhelming victory for the United States. William Henry Harrison secured U.S. control of Detroit and Amherstburg for the duration of the war. The War of 1812 continued for another full year before it ended with the Treaty of Ghent, which was signed on December 24, 1814. Native America was not represented at the negotiations for the settlement. The treaty established the *status quo ante bellum*; no territorial changes were made by either the United States or Great Britain. The native nations did not regain any of their lost homelands, and the following decades continued the processes of American Indian dispossession and U.S. expansionism.

Three U.S. figures intimately connected with the War of 1812 went on to use their wartime notoriety to reach the highest offices in the country. Colonel Andrew Jackson of the Tennessee militia led U.S. soldiers and various American Indian allies against the Red Stick Creeks, whose war was inspired by Tecumseh's visit and message to the Creek nation. On March 27, 1814, Jackson defeated the Red Stick Creeks at the Battle of Horseshow Bend, and on August 9, 1814, he forced the Creeks to sign the Treaty of Fort Jackson, which ceded 23 million acres of Creek land—including land belonging to Jackson's Creek allies—to the United States. Jackson's reputation as a war hero and "Indian fighter" propelled him to the U.S. presidency in both 1828 and 1832. Jackson went on to be the architect of the Indian Removal Act and the force behind the Trail of Tears and the dispossession of the so-called Civilized Tribes.

Colonel Richard Johnson of the Kentucky Volunteers led the cavalry charge at the Battle of the Thames. He claimed to be responsible for the death of Tecumseh, leading to the popular chorus "Ripsey Rampsey, Rumpsey Dumpsey, Colonel Johnson Shot Tecumseh." The claim, although uncertain, brought him a great deal of national attention. He used this fame to political advantage as he moved from the Kentucky legislature to the U.S. House of Representatives and the U.S. Senate. He became vice president under President Martin Van Buren in 1836. During Van Buren's and Johnson's single term in office, the United States began the forced removal of the southeastern native nations.

William Henry Harrison, territorial governor of Indiana and Commander of the Army of the Northwest, architect of the Treaty of Fort Wayne, and victor of the Battles of Tippecanoe and the Thames, grew famous as the man who had burned Prophetstown and defeated Tecumseh. He campaigned for office as "Tippecanoe" and served in the Ohio legislature, the U.S. House of Representatives, and the U.S. Senate. He also held the position of Minister to Colombia from 1828 to 1829. He was defeated by Martin Van Buren in the presidential election of 1836, but he won the White House four years later. Because he had leaned so heavily on his war record during the campaign, he felt compelled to prove his stamina and fighting spirit on the day of his inauguration. He delivered his address—the longest inaugural address in U.S. history—without a coat in the cold and rain and then rode through the streets for the inaugural parade. He caught a cold, which developed into pneumonia and pleurisy. He died on April 4, 1841, after one month and eleven hours in office.

Harrison's untimely death, on the heels of his campaign as "Tippecanoe," fueled a legend that has helped to keep Tecumseh alive in popular memory, even though it has no basis in fact. The story asserts that the Prophet, after the death of his brother, cursed his foe, William Henry Harrison. This curse not only followed him to the White House but plagued successive presidents, as well. The curse ensured that Harrison died in office and that every president after him who won the election in a year ending in "0" also would perish. This 20-year cycle did hold for 120 years. Harrison (elected in 1840) died in office of illness; Abraham Lincoln (1860) was assassinated while in office; James Garfield (1880) was assassinated while in office; William McKinley (1900) was assassinated while in office; Warren Harding (1920) died of a heart attack while in office; Franklin Roosevelt (1940) died of a cerebral hemorrhage while in office; and John F. Kennedy (1960) was assassinated while in office. Ronald Reagan (1980) did not die while president, but he was gravely wounded in an assassination attempt while in office. George W. Bush (2000) apparently broke the "curse," but this certainly has not banished the cycle, or its alleged cause, from public memory. Even at the time of Harrison's shocking death, writers and speakers invoked Tecumseh's memory, proving how closely the lives and legacies of these two men were bound.

NOTES

1. Quoted in John Sudgen, *Tecumseh: A Life* (New York: Henry Holt, 1997), p. 341.

2. Ibid., pp. 340–341.

3. Quoted in "Documents, Artefacts and Imagery," *Military Subjects: War of 1812 Magazine*, Issue 2 (February 2006). Available at http://www.napoleon-series. org/military/Warof1812/2006/Issue2/c_abos.html. Also quoted in C. F. Klinck, ed., *Tecumseh: Fact and Fiction in Early Records* (Ottawa: Tecumseh Press, 1978), pp. 184–185.

Chapter 9

TECUMSEH IN MEMORY AND POPULAR CULTURE

Certainly Tecumseh remained an inspiration to Native American movements in both the United States and Canada and is invoked to this day as the symbol of indigenous resistance and pan-tribal unity. His appeal, however, transcended the boundaries of American Indian political activism. During his life, many Anglos were fascinated by him, even as others feared him. In death, he became a romanticized object of fantasy as well as the revered embodiment of principled leadership.

Tecumseh was memorialized and mythologized almost from the moment of his death. In 1818, Lieutenant Francis Hall, a British officer, published a poem in memory of a man he clearly admired. "To the Memory of Tecumseh" exemplifies many such tributes to the tragic chief:

Tecumseh has no grave, but eagles dipt
Their rav'ning beaks, and drank his stout heart's tide,
Leaving his bones to whiten where he died:
His skin by Christian tomahawks was stript
From the bar'd fibres.—Impotence of pride!
Triumphant o'er the earth-worm, but in vain
Deeming th'impassive spirit to deride,
Which, nothing or immortal, knows no pain!
Might we torment him to this earth again,
That were an agony: his children's blood
Delug'd his soul, and, like a fiery flood,
Scorch'd up his core of being. Then the stain
Of flight was on him, and the wringing thought.
He should no more the crimson hatchet raise,

Nor drink from kindred lips his song of praise;
So Liberty, he deemed, with life was cheaply bought.[1]

Perhaps part of his appeal lay in the fact that he conformed to mainstream white conceptions of the noble savage. Popular contemporary accounts emphasized the fact he was illiterate, for example, and not that he
was multilingual. His talents for eloquent oratory and military strategy
suggested parallels with other nonChristian heroes of the Christianized
West, such as the Greeks and Romans. His inherent good looks and noble
bearing perhaps even elicited comparisons with ideas of humanity before
the Fall. He also appeared to conform to a strict moral system of behavior
and insisted that his followers do likewise. This code of honesty and forth-
rightness in dealings with other parties, of protection to the innocent and
mercy to the helpless, was reminiscent of the code of chivalry; indeed, like
a knight out of a fairy tale, Tecumseh was termed "chivalrous" in innu-
merable reflections on his life. His efforts on behalf of unifying, defending,
and bettering his people reminded some of his admirers of the premodern
hero King Arthur.

But, although British and U.S. culture found worthy attributes in Tecumseh's life—or, at least, his legend—he was undeniably Other, and all
the more exotic and romantic because of this. In his *The Life of Tecumseh
and of His Brother the Prophet* (1841), Benjamin Drake quoted Judge James
Hall on Tecumseh: "He was called the Napoleon of the west; and so far
as that title was deserved by splendid genius, unwavering courage, untir-
ing perseverance, boldness of conception and promptitude of action, it
was fairly bestowed upon this accomplished savage."[2] These descriptions
fit Tecumseh, but he was not a Napoleon, or any leader the whites could
understand.

In a system of decentralized communities, in which warriors could create or defect to other villages and leaders maintained their authority at the
pleasure of their people, Tecumseh did not seek to consolidate power for
personal gain or the accumulation of wealth. He won and kept the loyalty
of his followers essentially by becoming their servant. He was known for
his generosity to and protection of his people. At the height of his power,
he owned only what he could fit in his saddlebags and ate and slept on
the open land or thanks to the hospitality of others. His invitation to Native American to follow him was far less about self-aggrandizement than
about liberating the warriors, harnessing their energy, and undermining
the weak or corrupt chiefs who enabled U.S. expansionism. The confederacy he championed was not an empire in the making, and Tecumseh
was not a Caesar.

One thing is certain: the first consumers of literature about Tecumseh possessed a boundless appetite. In the nineteenth century, Tecumseh generated more biographies, historical novels, verse romances, and epic poetry than any other Native American. Even those works represented as true stories often took great liberties with the facts. Some authors emphasized Tecumseh's similarities with other great Native American leaders such as Pontiac. Others "assimilated" him, depicting romances with white women and underscoring the parallels between his story and those of classic characters from European history and mythology. Still more writers focused on Tecumseh as a tragic hero, a casualty of the North American West.

John Richardson, who gained fame as Canada's first novelist, fought with Tecumseh at his final battle at Moraviantown before writing about him. In 1828, he penned a verse epic titled *Tecumseh: A Poem in Four Cantos*, which presented a portrait of Tecumseh as a self-sacrificing republican hero who, at the end, welcomed his own tragic demise. James Strange French's 1836 novel, *Elkswatawa; or, The Prophet of the West*, compared Tecumseh to Hannibal, the Roman military strategist who is often considered one of the greatest commanders in human history. Richard Emmon's 1836 play *Tecumseh; or, The Battle of the Thames, A National Drama* considered Tecumseh's chivalric values and humane sensibilities—something of an irony, since it was commissioned as campaign propaganda in support of then-Senator Richard Johnson, the man who claimed to have shot this paragon of virtue. William Galloway's 1934 *Old Chillicothe: Shawnee and Pioneer History* distilled earlier folklore about Tecumseh, and the legends he recounted remain the inspiration for a historical drama still performed today in Chillicothe, Ohio. According to this tale, Tecumseh fell in love with Rebecca Galloway, a white girl, who partially succeeded in Anglicizing him, before losing him to his destiny. Galloway overtly compared Tecumseh to Hamlet in his promise and tragedy.

The public thirst for stories about Tecumseh continued into the twentieth century. Between 1930 and 1939, the German author Fritz Steuben published an eight-book series of novels about Tecumseh's life, for example. Tecumseh and the Prophet play key roles in Alan W. Eckert's 1967 novel *The Frontiersmen: A Narrative*. James Alexander Thom published his novel about Tecumseh, *Panther in the Sky*, in 1989; in 1995, it was adapted into the TNT original film *Tecumseh, The Last Warrior*. As the fictional retellings of Tecumseh's life continued, important scholarly works of history about Tecumseh also appeared. As the fields of history, ethnohistory, and Native American studies have matured, academics have found new tools to employ in uncovering and understanding the life, times, and impact of the Shawnee chief.

The tragedy of Tecumseh's story has led to a noteworthy phenomenon in popular culture: Tecumseh is well remembered and represented in the genre of science fiction. Works of science fiction by definition ask the question "What if?," and it seems as though many authors have found it valuable to speculate about this question with reference to Tecumseh's life. This may be in part because Tecumseh's dream of a unified Native America with control over traditional homelands is still a dream pursued by individuals and organizations today, and science fiction works have allowed authors to theorize different responses to the query "What would Tecumseh do?" In fact, one of the first alternate histories ever written, Guy Dent's 1926 *The Emperor of the If*, involved Tecumseh.

Vine Deloria, Jr., published the speculative short story "Why the U.S. Never Fought the Indians" in 1976, imagining a world in which Tecumseh had united all of Native America into the Coalition of Indian Nations, which in turn opposed both Great Britain and the United States in the War of 1812 and became a power broker at the peace negotiations in Ghent. Beth Meacham's 1993 short story "One by One" explored how the Northwest Territory's history would have been different if Tecumseh had prevailed against Harrison at the Battle of the Thames. Other science fiction novels, such as L. Neil Smith's *Probability Broach* (1981), Orson Scott Card's ongoing *The Tales of Alvin Maker* series (1987-present), and Eric Flint's *1812: The Rivers of War* (2005), also contain alternate histories for Tecumseh. Furthermore, the science fiction television series *Star Trek: Deep Space Nine* (1993–1999) repeatedly referred to an Excelsior-class starship named *U.S.S. Tecumseh*.

Tecumseh's name appears on more than fictional starships. Four ships in the U.S. Navy have carried the name, the first in 1863. A naval reserve unit in Calgary, Alberta, is the HMCS Tecumseh, as well. Places named after the Shawnee chief include the following: Tecumseh, Kansas; Tecumseh, Michigan; Tecumseh, Missouri; Tecumseh, Nebraska; Tecumseh, Oklahoma; Tecumseh, Ontario; New Tecumseth, Ontario; and Mount Tecumseh in New Hampshire. Like his friend and ally Isaac Brock, Tecumseh is remembered by Canadians with various monuments as a hero who saved Canada from U.S. invasion.

Tecumseh also is widely associated with a statue on the grounds of the U.S. Naval Academy at Annapolis. The original wooden monument erected in 1866 was the figurehead of the U.S.S. *Delaware*. It represented not Tecumseh but rather the Delaware chief Tamanend. However, the cadets at the institution regularly assumed it was Tecumseh, because he was the most famous American Indian they knew, not to mention an excellent example of a warrior and leader. The name and identity stuck.

A bronze bust replaced the wooden one in 1930, and today the monument is officially regarded as a symbol of the Shawnee chief.

Through poems, plays, novels, films, and monuments, the Shawnee chief continues to live in popular memory and culture, claimed by the United States and Canada, as well as by Native America. The truth of Tecumseh remains more complex and more elusive than the facts of Tecumseh. Whether the image of "the Indian" or the diplomatic practitioner of *realpolitik*, the dedicated servant of unity or the practical artist of compromise, the principled champion of peace or the terrible instrument of war, Tecumseh will continue to be the object of study, speculation, and inspiration. His story is as much myth as history, and his mystery and message will challenge those who would learn more of and from him.

NOTES

1. Quoted in C. F. Klinck, ed., *Tecumseh: Fact and Fiction in Early Records* (Ottawa: Tecumseh Press, 1978), p. 221.

2. Quoted in Gordon M. Sayre, *The Indian Chief as Tragic Hero: Native Resistance and the Literatures of America, from Moctezuma to Tecumseh* (Chapel Hill: University of North Carolina Press, 2005), p. 269.

BIBLIOGRAPHY

BOOKS AND ARTICLES

Deloria, Jr., Vine. "Why the U.S. Never Fought the Indians." *Christian Century* 93 (January 7–14, 1976): 9–12.

Dowd, Gregory Evans. *A Spirited Resistance: The North American Indian Struggle for Unity, 1745–1815*. Baltimore: Johns Hopkins University Press, 1992.

Eckert, Alan W. *The Frontiersmen: A Narrative*. Boston: Little, Brown, 1967.

Edmunds, R. David. *The Shawnee Prophet*. Lincoln: University of Nebraska Press, 1983.

———. *Tecumseh and the Quest for Indian Leadership*. New York: Longman, 1984.

Eggleston, Edgar, and Elizabeth Eggleston Seelye. *Tecumseh and the Shawnee Prophet*. New York: Dodd, Mead, 1878.

Gilbert, Bil. *God Gave Us This Country: Tekamthi and the First American Civil War*. New York: Anchor Books, 1990.

Horsman, Reginald. *Matthew Elliott, British Indian Agent*. Detroit: Wayne State University Press, 1964.

Hunter, John D. *Memoirs of a Captivity among the Indians of North America*, 3rd ed. London: n.p., 1824.

Josephy, Alvin M, Jr. *The Patriot Chiefs: A Chronicle of American Indian Leadership*. New York: Viking, 1961.

Klinck, C. F., ed. *Tecumseh: Fact and Fiction in Early Records*. Ottawa: Tecumseh Press, 1978.

Meacham, Beth. "One by One." In *Alternate Warriors*, ed. Mike Resnick. New York: Tor, 1993. 307–323.

Nichols, Roger L. *American Indians in U.S. History*. Norman: University of Oklahoma Press, 2003.

St-Denis, Guy. *Tecumseh's Bones*. Montreal: McGill-Queen's University Press, 2005.

Sayre, Gordon M. *The Indian Chief as Tragic Hero: Native Resistance and the Literatures of America, from Moctezuma to Tecumseh*. Chapel Hill: University of North Carolina Press, 2005.

Sturgis, Amy H. "Florida's Forgotten Rebels: Rediscovering the Most Successful Slave Revolt in American History." *Reason* (April 2007): 54–57.

———. *The Trail of Tears and Indian Removal*. Westport, CT: Greenwood Press, 2006.

Sudgen, John. *Tecumseh: A Life*. New York: Henry Holt, 1997.

Handbook of Texas Online, s.v. "Big Jim," http://www.tsha.utexas.edu/handbook/online/articles/BB/fbi5.html.

INTERNET SOURCES

"Documents, Artefacts and Imagery." *Military Subjects: War of 1812 Magazine*, Issue 2 (February 2006). The Napoleon Series. http://www.napoleon-series.org/military/Warof1812/2006/Issue2/c_abos.html.

Handbook of Texas Online, s.v. Texas State Historical Association. http://www.tsha.utexas.edu/handbook/online/articles/BB/fbi5.html.

Tippecanoe Battlefield. Tippecanoe County Historical Association. http://www.tcha.mus.in.us/battlefield.htm.

"Treaties between the United States and Native Americans." *The Avalon Project at Yale Law School*. http://www.yale.edu/lawweb/avalon/ntreaty/ntreaty.htm.

"Treaty with the Delawares, Etc., 1809." *Indiana Historical Bureau*. http://www.statelib.lib.in.us/www/ihb/resources/docdelawares.html.

INDEX

About the Author

AMY H. STURGIS is Assistant Professor of Interdisciplinary Studies at Belmont University. She earned her Ph.D. in Intellectual History at Vanderbilt University. She has authored or edited seven books and written numerous chapters and articles in both Native American and science fiction/fantasy studies, including *The Trail of Tears and Indian Removal* (Greenwood, 2006), *Presidents from Hayes through McKinley, 1877–1901* (Greenwood, 2003), and *Presidents from Washington through Monroe, 1789–1825* (Greenwood, 2001).

CPSIA information can be obtained
at www.ICGtesting.com
Printed in the USA
BVHW04*0920160718
521333BV00048B/259/P

9 780313 341779